SKINNY SAUCES

& MARINADES

by ERICA LEVY KLEIN

Surrey Books

CHICAGO

SKINNY SAUCES & MARINADES is published by Surrey Books, Inc.
230 E. Ohio St., Suite 120, Chicago, IL 60611.

First edition: 1 2 3 4 5

This book is manufactured in the United States of America.

Library of Congress Cataloging-in-Publication data:

Klein, Erica Levy.
    Skinny sauces & marinades / by Erica Levy Klein. — 1st ed.
    140p.   cm. — (Skinny cookbooks series)
    Includes bibliographical references and index.
    ISBN 0-940625-87-3 (cloth): $20.95   ISBN 0-940625-83-0 (pbk.): $12.95
    1. Low-fat diet—Recipes. 2. Sauces. 3. Marinades. I. Title.
II. Title: Skinny sauces and marinades. III. Series.
RM237.7.K583 1994
641.5'638—dc20   94-8527
                                                                                                                          CIP

Editorial and production. *Bookcrafters, Inc., Chicago*
Art Director: *Hughes & Co., Chicago*
Cover and interior illustrations by *Laurel DiGangi*
Back cover photos courtesy *California Olive Industry*

For free catalog and prices on quantity purchases, contact Surrey Books at the
address above.

This title is distributed to the trade by Publishers Group West.

Other titles in the "Skinny" Cookbooks Series:

Skinny Beef	*Skinny Pizzas*
Skinny Chicken	*Skinny Potatoes*
Skinny Chocolate	*Skinny Seafood*
Skinny Cookies, Cakes & Sweets	*Skinny Soups*
Skinny One-Pot Meals	*Skinny Spices*
Skinny Pasta	

For
Clay, Beth, and Taylor,
with quiet love

CONTENTS

FOREWORD

S ome people collect antiques; others, matchbooks. And still others accumulate souvenirs from exciting travels at home and abroad.

I fall into the latter category, although for reasons my therapist still struggles to understand, all of my travels qualify as "culinary adventures."

Along with one of the world's largest collections of exotic herbs and spices lugged home from overseas (hence, my first cookbook in this series, *Skinny Spices*), I am always purchasing just one more souvenir sauce to add to my ever-expanding collection. The only time I've regretted buying "just one more sauce" was when my incendiary Thai pepper marinade sandwiched itself between all the other sauce bottles in my luggage, exploded inside the suitcase, and turned every item of clothing I owned a bright shade of chili red.

Of course, I don't just purchase *any* sauce. After all, I've got standards. I only buy the low-fat kind that I can guiltlessly slather all over healthy food while still maintaining the illusion of being supremely virtuous.

I guess you could say that I've joined the ranks of the Sauce Obsessed—an addiction for which there is no twelve-step program as yet. Sauces fill every shelf of the pantry cupboard, overflow all our cabinets, and occupy so many nooks and crannies in our dining room that my husband insists we will soon own the world's first crystal chandelier constructed entirely of glass sauce jars.

Which is why I was so delighted (and my husband so relieved) when Susan Schwartz, the publisher of Surrey Books, asked me to research and write *Skinny Sauces and Marinades*. I, of course, was eager to finally write a cookbook about my delicious pursuit of sauces from around the globe. But my husband was even more ecstatic. He realized that in order to have enough space to analyze, cook, and test new sauces and marinades, I probably would have to get rid of some we already had.

In writing this book, I am especially indebted to my nutritional research consultant, Mickey Kitterman. Mickey helped me refine the recipes, culled from around the world, that accompany all 48 sauces, constantly looking for more and better ways to reduce fat, calories, and sodium while never compromising taste. It is to Mickey's culinary genius (and my husband's infinite patience with my sauce collection) that I dedicate this "skinny" volume of mouthwatering, soul-satisfying recipes.

Erica Levy Klein

COOKING BY THE NUMBERS

A lthough nutritional information is provided for each recipe in this book, you should remember that nutritional data is rarely—if ever—infallible. The sizes of vegetables and fruits may vary; the nutritional labels on packaged foods may have a plus or minus 20 percent error factor; and cooking techniques and appliances can all affect nutritional results.

Please also note that when you see the phrase "salt and pepper to taste," it means these ingredients are optional and are not figured into the nutritional analyses. And when there are two choices for ingredients, such as "chicken, *or* fish stock," the *first* listed item is the one used to develop the nutritional data.

If you have any health problem that mandates strict dietary requirements, it is important that you consult a physician, clinical dietitian, or nutritionist before proceeding with any recipe in this book. However, you can use the nutritional data as a starting point, and we hope you will find it useful for planning delicious and memorable meals.

1.
SKINNY SECRETS FROM THE WORLD'S GREAT SAUCE CHEFS

What has 100 calories, countless grams of fat, and can add up pounds more quickly than a British accountant?

It's one lone tablespoon of a typical creamy sauce, the kind that comes in the flavors we all know and love—flavors like "butter," "chocolate," and every child's favorite, "cheese."

Relatively harmless in small quantities, these sauces have a way of being overused to do everything from making vegetables more palatable to masking humble (or even rapidly aging) ingredients.

Unfortunately these rich sauces, and others based on butter and cream, have been repeatedly linked to serious health problems such as obesity, high cholesterol, and diet-related cancers. Clearly, it is no longer a smart choice (or a very popular one) to cling to the Ghost of Sauces Past.

The good news is that the inventiveness of top chefs around the country has resulted in something of a light sauce revolution. Today's sauces go easy on the fat and calories but miraculously manage to retain all the taste, flavor, and texture of their rich predecessors. It is now perfectly acceptable to substitute vegetable purees or evaporated skim milk for cream in a creamy sauce. It's OK to sauté or marinate meat or fish in fruit juice, vinegar, or wine. It's just fine to dissolve cornstarch in a little stock or water as a low-fat thickener instead of the classic flour and butter combination.

And that's where *Skinny Sauces and Marinades* can be especially useful to you. On one level, it's a comprehensive guide to low-fat, healthy sauce-making techniques. But this book also offers 96 quick, easy recipes that use the sauces (including dessert sauces) to make meals more delicious and visually appealing. The non-dessert sauces are all extremely versatile and can add exciting new dimensions to chicken, beef, seafood, lean pork, vegetables, pasta, rice, and potatoes.

On the following pages, you'll get all the "skinny" secrets of the great sauce chefs in one convenient place and be able to make entrees, appetizers, side dishes, and desserts that are so good they qualify as downright seductive. It is my fond hope that this latest addition to your culinary collection will make it possible to do what you've always wanted—have your sauce and eat it too!

2.
Skinny (but Delicious) Low-Fat Substitutes

I *nstead of* heavy cream try reconstituted non-fat dry milk made extra strength. Use ½ cup of milk powder to make 1 cup of milk.

Instead of a butter and flour roux consider thickening sauces with pureed vegetables such as butternut squash, onions, potatoes, parsnips, or turnips.

Instead of egg yolks switch to egg whites or a mixture of ¼ yolks to ¾ whites.

Instead of whole milk substitute skim milk or a mixture of yogurt, water, and a drop or two of sweetener.

Instead of butter on your popcorn use a butter-flavored non-stick spray.

Instead of chocolate experiment with cocoa powder—it contains little or no fat.

Instead of a creamy soup as a sauce base lighten up by chilling low-sodium chicken stock in the freezer for one hour until you can skim the fat right off the top. Heat, add herbs and a generous dollop of yogurt to thicken.

Instead of relying on oil or butter for flavor add tomato juice, fruit juice, vinegars, defatted stock, or vegetable cooking liquid.

Instead of flour substitute cornstarch or arrowroot, since they have twice the thickening power.

Instead of drowning a salad in a creamy salad dressing, spray your salad first with olive-oil-flavored non-stick cooking spray. Then dip your fork into a little salad dressing on the side with each mouthful.

And one final "Skinny Sauces" tip… If cholesterol isn't a problem, one egg can thicken one cup of liquid to the consistency of a medium-thick sauce. Add the egg very slowly, a tablespoon at a time, to heated liquid. To prevent curdling, cook over reduced heat.

3.
GETTING THE SKINNY ON HERBS AND SPICES

The right spice or herb can liven up just about any sauce without adding fat or calories. Here is a brief guide to how to use dried herbs and spices (sparingly) to zip up sauces and win raves from your family and friends:

♦ *allspice*   its scent is reminiscent of cinnamon, cloves, and nutmeg "all" rolled into one. Powerful, so use lightly. Especially good in curry sauces.

♦ *anise*   a sweet, licorice-like taste that's terrific when used in moderation. Toast the seeds first in a little oil.

♦ *basil*   sweet and pungent; great in garlicky, tomato-based sauces and in Thai sauces. Good in marinades, too.

- ◆ **bay leaf** a strong taste that adds depth and texture to ordinary sauces and stews.
- ◆ **caraway** has a mild, tangy quality that's similar to dill seed.
- ◆ **cardamon** (also spelled **cardamom**) sharp, pungent, and sweet, with a cinnamonlike aroma. Good as an addition to sweet sauces since it allows cutting back on sugar.
- ◆ **cayenne pepper** the tongue-searing red pepper that adds a kick to Creole, Cajun, and Tex-Mex sauces.
- ◆ **celery seeds** celery-like flavor that zips up salad dressings and coleslaw.
- ◆ **chervil leaf** a strong, herbal taste with just a hint of tarragon. Great with fish or sauces that accompany fish.
- ◆ **chives** a mild onion taste that can be incorporated into sauces or used as a colorful garnish.
- ◆ **cilantro** also known as Chinese parsley and coriander leaf. Better and more flavorful in its fresh form, although some people may suffer an allergic reaction. A natural addition to Asian or Mexican soups.
- ◆ **cinnamon** sweet, fragrant, and versatile enough to spice up everything from curry sauces to dessert sauces.
- ◆ **cloves** a type of evergreen bud typically found in pungent marinades or sweet sauces.
- ◆ **coriander** in its seed form, spicy and citrus-like. Good in chili or delicate sauces.
- ◆ **cumin** the major flavor ingredient in most chili powders. Good in Indian or Latin American dishes. Blends especially well with yogurt.
- ◆ **dill weed** the feathery leaf of the dill plant, with a pungent kick and light, heady fragrance. Wonderful in lemon-based sauces.
- ◆ **fennel seed** a licorice taste similar to anise but much milder. Use sparingly so as not to overpower a sauce.
- ◆ **fenugreek** spicy, slightly bitter maple-like flavor typically found in more authentic curry sauces.
- ◆ **garlic** a flavor enhancer for just about any sauce. New varieties like Dr. Sakai's Garlic will even leave your breath smelling sweet! Use sparingly to add dimension; add more to increase garlicky kick.
- ◆ **ginger** a sharp, spicy-sweet flavor that wakes up Asian dishes and adds a pleasing taste to sweet sauces.
- ◆ **horseradish** a white root powder with a hot, hearty flavor. The powder is even more intense than the prepared bottled variety, so exercise caution. *Wasabi* is a particular green type of hot horseradish favored by the Japanese.

- ♦ ***mace***   the ground outer covering of nutmeg, with a more compelling, pungent fragrance.

- ♦ ***marjoram***   a milder cousin of oregano. Good for creating a Mediterranean taste.

- ♦ ***mint***   light, fragrant, and tangy at the same time. A good counterpoint to garlic, or use it to add a pleasing contrast in sweet sauces.

- ♦ ***mustard powder***   hot and spicy; a tangy addition to salad dressings and marinades and essential to authentic vinaigrette.

- ♦ ***nutmeg***   mild, nutty, and fragrant. Good in cheese-based sauces or dessert sauces.

- ♦ ***oregano***   the dominant herb in most spaghetti and pizza sauces.

- ♦ ***paprika***   a mild, ground reddish pepper that's delicious as an addition to creamier sauces.

- ♦ ***parsley***   the ever-present garnish, with a mild herbal flavor that sometimes is hard to distinguish from other ingredients.

- ♦ ***pepper***   a spicy berry with many varieties including black, green, pink and white. Use the latter in white sauces.

- ♦ ***poppy seed***   tiny seeds with a sweetish, nutty taste and texture. Wonderful in coleslaw and sweet sauces.

- ♦ ***rosemary***   fragrant, strongly flavored leaf that looks like a miniature pine needle. Remove from sauces before serving to avoid puncturing the mouth or tongue.

- ♦ ***saffron***   the most expensive of all spices because of the number of flowers needed to obtain a small amount. A traditional accompaniment for many Indian, Spanish, and Mediterranean dishes.

- ♦ ***sage***   strong, pleasant flavor with a sweet, herbal fragrance.

- ♦ ***savory***   a mild, thyme-like taste that adds special fragrance to sauces.

- ♦ ***sesame seed***   mild, nut-like flavor that improves with roasting in a little oil first. Use as a major ingredient or a pleasing garnish.

- ♦ ***tarragon leaf***   a rich, sweet flavor faintly reminiscent of anise. Good with sauces to accompany chicken.

- ♦ ***thyme***   distinctive, pleasant herbal flavor and fragrance that's wonderful in tomato-based sauces or salad dressings.

- ♦ ***turmeric***   a brilliant yellow ground spice with a peppery aroma and ginger-like flavor. Adds the golden color to curry powder.

4.
FRENCH SAUCES AND MARINADES

Honey Dijon Sauce

♦

Caramelized Onion Sauce

♦

Light and Creamy Dill Sauce

♦

Tarragon Mustard Sauce

♦

Tomato Dill Sauce

♦

Sherry Herb Garden Sauce

♦

Orange Sage Sauce

HONEY DIJON SAUCE

Yield 5 cups *(20 quarter-cup servings)*

- 3 cups defatted chicken stock
- 1 cup Dijon mustard
- 1 cup honey
- ¼ cup shallots, minced
- 1 tablespoon paprika
- 1 tablespoon cornstarch dissolved in ¼ cup white wine

Bring the first 5 ingredients to boil and simmer 15 minutes. Thicken with cornstarch and wine mixture, and simmer another 5 minutes.

Nutritional Data

PER SERVING:		EXCHANGES:	
Calories:	72	Milk:	0.0
Fat (gm):	0.8	Vegetable:	0.3
Sat. fat (gm):	0.8	Fruit:	0.8
Cholesterol (mg):	0	Bread:	0.0
Sodium (mg):	274	Meat:	0.0
% Calories from fat:	5	Fat:	0.2

HAM-AND-SPINACH-STUFFED CHICKEN BREAST
with Honey Dijon Sauce

Serves 6

6　boneless chicken breasts, skin removed
6　thin slices of low-fat ham
1　bunch spinach
　　toothpicks
2　cups *Honey Dijon Sauce*

Place chicken breasts flat on cutting board and pound lightly with meat mallet or can wrapped in foil. Top each breast with ham slice. Lay spinach leaves across ham completely covering it. Roll up breasts jellyroll style and secure with toothpicks.

Roast in 375-degree oven approximately 20-30 minutes until juice runs clear. Slice into pinwheels or serve whole atop ¼ cup Honey Dijon Sauce.

Nutritional Data

PER SERVING:

Calories:	237
Fat (gm):	3.7
Sat. fat (gm):	1
Cholesterol (mg):	81.7
Sodium (mg):	790
% Calories from fat:	14

EXCHANGES:

Milk:	0.0	Bread:	0.0
Veg.:	0.6	Meat:	0.4
Fruit:	0.7	Fat:	0.1

HONEY-GLAZED PORK CHOPS
with Honey Dijon Sauce

Serves 6

6　extra-lean butterflied pork loin chops, marinated (see recipe below)
1¾　cups *Honey Dijon Sauce*
　　Non-stick cooking spray

Marinade

¼　cup honey
¼　cup white wine
¼　tablespoon black pepper, coarsely ground
2　tablespoons low-sodium soy sauce

Nutritional Data

PER SERVING:

Calories:	274
Fat (gm):	23.9
Sat. fat (gm):	9.3
Cholesterol (mg):	100
Sodium (mg):	420
% Calories from fat:	30

EXCHANGES:

Milk:	0.0	Bread:	0.4
Veg.:	0.0	Meat:	4.0
Fruit:	2.0	Fat:	2.1

Mix together Marinade ingredients and marinate pork chops at least 1 hour. Preheat oven to 350 degrees. Drain pork chops and reserve Marinade.

After preparing non-stick skillet with cooking spray, brown chops on all sides. Place browned chops in porcelain baking dish and pour in reserved Marinade.

Bake at 350 degrees 25-30 minutes until chops are cooked thoroughly. Glaze with ¼ cup Honey Dijon Sauce.

CARAMELIZED ONION SAUCE

Yield 5 cups (10 half-cup servings)

2 cups onions, thinly sliced
  Non-stick cooking spray
1 tablespoon sugar
1 cup port wine
2 cups defatted chicken stock
  Salt and pepper to taste

C oat non-stick skillet with cooking spray and brown onion slices 5 minutes on medium-high heat. Stir and flip onions constantly so they do not scorch. Add sugar and lower heat immediately, continuing to let onions brown and caramelize 5 more minutes, stirring often.

Add port wine, and increase heat to high until boiling wine is reduced by half. Add stock and simmer 1 hour. Salt and pepper to taste.

Nutritional Data

PER SERVING:		EXCHANGES:	
Calories:	42	Milk:	0.0
Fat (gm):	0.3	Vegetable:	0.4
Sat. fat (gm):	0.1	Fruit:	0.1
Cholesterol (mg):	0	Bread:	0.0
Sodium (mg):	157	Meat:	0.0
% Calories from fat:	7	Fat:	0.3

VEAL SCALOPPINI
with Caramelized Onion Sauce

Serves 6

12 large, thinly-sliced pieces of veal
   (scaloppini style)
1 cup flour
1 tablespoon pepper
1 tablespoon paprika
1 tablespoon garlic salt
   Non-stick cooking spray
2 cups *Caramelized Onion Sauce*

Nutritional Data

PER SERVING:

Calories:	269
Fat (gm):	10.2
Sat. fat (gm):	3.9
Cholesterol (mg):	66.9
Sodium (mg):	144
% Calories from fat:	30

EXCHANGES:

Milk:	0.0	Bread:	0.9
Veg.:	0.2	Meat:	2.3
Fruit:	0.1	Fat:	0.8

Combine flour and spices in paper bag and shake well to mix. Dredge veal in seasoned flour and shake off excess. Coat non-stick skillet with cooking spray, and brown veal in small batches for approximately 2 minutes per side. Serve atop ¼ cup of Caramelized Onion Sauce.

MARINATED AND GRILLED FLANK STEAK
with Caramelized Onion Sauce

Serves 8

2½ lbs. extra-lean flank steak
   Marinade (see recipe below)
2 cups *Caramelized Onion Sauce*

Marinade

1 cup red wine
2 large cloves garlic, minced
¼ cup red wine vinegar
1 bay leaf
1 small onion, sliced
1 medium carrot, sliced
2 whole black peppercorns
2 sprigs fresh parsley

Nutritional Data

PER SERVING:

Calories:	299
Fat (gm):	8.7
Sat. fat (gm):	3.4
Cholesterol (mg):	82.5
Sodium (mg):	152
% Calories from fat:	30

EXCHANGES:

Milk:	0.1	Bread:	0.0
Veg.:	0.2	Meat:	3.5
Fruit:	0.0	Fat:	0.4

Combine all ingredients for Marinade and bring to rolling boil. Cool Marinade, pour over flank steak, and marinate steak overnight, turning 2 times.

Remove steak from Marinade. Grill flank steak, turning once after 4 minutes for medium-rare meat. Slice in thin strips across the grain, and serve over ¼ cup Caramelized Onion Sauce.

LIGHT AND CREAMY DILL SAUCE

Yield 3 cups (6 half-cup servings)

2 cups fish stock, *or* defatted chicken stock
1 clove garlic, minced
¼ cup onion, minced
1½ tablespoons cornstarch dissolved in ½ cup white wine
¼ cup evaporated skim milk
¼ cup fresh dill
Juice of 1 lemon
Salt and pepper to taste

C ombine stock, garlic, and onion and simmer 5 minutes. Thicken with cornstarch and wine mixture while stirring constantly. Add milk and dill, and continue to simmer 1-2 minutes without boiling. Remove from heat and add lemon juice. Add salt and pepper to taste.

Nutritional Data

PER SERVING:		EXCHANGES:	
Calories:	48	Milk:	0.1
Fat (gm):	0.5	Vegetable:	0.1
Sat. fat (gm):	0.2	Fruit:	0.1
Cholesterol (mg):	0.4	Bread:	0.1
Sodium (mg):	273	Meat:	0.0
% Calories from fat:	10	Fat:	0.3

DILLED SEA SCALLOPS
with Spinach Pasta

Serves 6

1½ lbs. sea scallops
3 cups *Light and Creamy Dill Sauce*
4 cups cooked spinach noodles
Lemon slices for garnish

Bring sauce to simmering point but do not boil. Add scallops and cook quickly until done, 3-4 minutes. Do not overcook since scallops will get tough after 4 minutes. Serve scallops and sauce over spinach noodles, and garnish with fresh lemon slices.

Nutritional Data

PER SERVING:

Calories:	290
Fat (gm):	3
Sat. fat (gm):	0.6
Cholesterol (mg):	73
Sodium (mg):	463
% Calories from fat:	9

EXCHANGES:

Milk:	0.1	Bread:	1.7
Veg.:	0.1	Meat:	0.0
Fruit:	0.1	Fat:	0.6

GRILLED CHICKEN STRIPS
with Light and Creamy Dill Sauce

Serves 6

1½ lbs. chicken strips, skin removed
1 cup low-fat Italian salad dressing, vinaigrette style
2 cups *Light and Creamy Dill Sauce*

Marinate chicken strips in Italian salad dressing at least 1 hour and preferably overnight. Grill chicken over hot coals or in the oven until done, about 2 minutes per side. Serve hot, drizzled with Light and Creamy Dill Sauce.

Nutritional Data

PER SERVING:

Calories:	214
Fat (gm):	5.9
Sat. fat (gm):	1.1
Cholesterol (mg):	66.1
Sodium (mg):	661
% Calories from fat:	25

EXCHANGES:

Milk:	0.1	Bread:	0.1
Veg.:	0.1	Meat:	2.9
Fruit:	0.1	Fat:	2.1

TARRAGON MUSTARD SAUCE

Yield 2 cups *(4 half-cup servings)*

1¼ cups low-sodium Dijon mustard
¼ cup fresh tarragon, finely minced
¼ cup onion, finely minced

ombine all ingredients and stir well. Refrigerate at least 1 hour before serving.

Nutritional Data

PER SERVING:		EXCHANGES:	
Calories:	69	Milk:	0.0
Fat (gm):	4.1	Vegetable:	1.4
Sat. fat (gm):	1.7	Fruit:	0.0
Cholesterol (mg):	0	Bread:	0.1
Sodium (mg):	582	Meat:	0.0
% Calories from fat:	20	Fat:	0.7

GRILLED CHICKEN BREASTS
with Tarragon Mustard Sauce

Serves 6

6 boneless chicken breasts, skin removed and marinated (see recipe below)

1½ cups *Tarragon Mustard Sauce*

Marinade

1 cup honey

¼ cup white wine

1 tablespoon fresh tarragon, finely minced

Nutritional Data			
PER SERVING:			
Calories:			300
Fat (gm):			4.8
Sat. fat (gm):			0.4
Cholesterol (mg):			34.2
Sodium (mg):			792
% Calories from fat:			13
EXCHANGES:			
Milk:	0.0	Bread:	0.1
Veg.:	1.4	Meat:	1.5
Fruit:	2.7	Fat:	0.8

Combine Marinade ingredients and marinate chicken 1-2 hours. Grill over hickory or mesquite briquettes if possible, or in oven at high heat until juices run clear. Serve with Tarragon Mustard Sauce as a savory accompaniment.

COUNTRY GLAZED HAM
with Apricots and Tarragon Mustard Sauce

Serves 6

2 cups apricots, diced

1 cup sherry

1 precooked light ham, about 2 lbs.

½ cup tarragon mustard

1 cup brown sugar

1 cup apricot nectar

1 cup *Tarragon Mustard Sauce*

Nutritional Data			
PER SERVING:			
Calories:			342
Fat (gm):			8.8
Sat. fat (gm):			2.5
Cholesterol (mg):			70.9
Sodium (mg):			771
% Calories from fat:			20
EXCHANGES:			
Milk:	0.0	Bread:	0.0
Veg.:	0.4	Meat:	3.5
Fruit:	2.3	Fat:	0.8

Soak apricots in sherry overnight.

Preheat oven to 350 degrees. Place ham in roasting pan, and coat entirely with tarragon mustard. Sprinkle brown sugar over top and sides, pour apricot nectar into pan, and bake 1 hour. Baste often.

Then add sherry-soaked apricots to pan and bake 30 minutes longer. Serve with Tarragon Mustard Sauce thinned by pan juices.

TOMATO DILL SAUCE

Yield 3 cups (6 half-cup servings)

1   large clove garlic, minced
½ cup shallots, minced
1   tablespoon olive oil
½ cup white wine
2   cups clam juice, *or* fish stock
1   cup diced tomato
1   tablespoon cornstarch dissolved in ¼ cup water
2   tablespoons fresh dill
    Salt and pepper to taste

Sauté garlic and shallots in olive oil until transparent but not browned. Add wine and clam juice and simmer 5 minutes. Add tomato and bring to rolling boil. Thicken with cornstarch and water mixture. Add dill and season with salt and pepper.

Nutritional Data

PER SERVING:		EXCHANGES:	
Calories:	92	Milk:	0.0
Fat (gm):	2.5	Vegetable:	0.7
Sat. fat (gm):	0.8	Fruit:	0.6
Cholesterol (mg):	0	Bread:	0.1
Sodium (mg):	326	Meat:	0.0
% Calories from fat:	23	Fat:	0.7

ORANGE ROUGHY
with Tomato Dill Sauce

Serves 6

6 orange roughy fillets
3 cups *Tomato Dill Sauce*

Place fish fillets in baking dish, and cover completely with Tomato Dill Sauce. Bake in 350-degree oven 20 minutes or until sauce is bubbly and fish is thoroughly cooked.

Nutritional Data

PER SERVING:

Calories:	142
Fat (gm):	3
Sat. fat (gm):	0.3
Cholesterol (mg):	14.7
Sodium (mg):	33
% Calories from fat:	19

EXCHANGES:

Milk:	0.0	Bread:	0.1
Veg.:	0.7	Meat:	0.9
Fruit:	0.6	Fat:	0.7

BROILED HALIBUT STEAK
with Tomato Dill "Butter"

Serves 6

6 halibut steaks
1 tablespoon olive oil
   Juice of 1 lemon
6 tablespoons diet margarine
3 cups *Tomato Dill Sauce*

Brush steaks with olive oil. Depending on thickness of fillets, broil approximately 4 minutes on each side. Squeeze fresh lemon juice over steaks and dot with margarine. Pour Tomato Dill Sauce over fillets to serve.

Nutritional Data

PER SERVING:

Calories:	214
Fat (gm):	10.7
Sat. fat (gm):	1.6
Cholesterol (mg):	14.7
Sodium (mg):	422
% Calories from fat:	22

EXCHANGES:

Milk:	0.0	Bread:	0.1
Veg.:	0.7	Meat:	0.9
Fruit:	0.7	Fat:	2.3

SHERRY HERB GARDEN SAUCE

◆

Yield 2 cups *(4 half-cup servings)*

2 cups defatted chicken stock, *or* fish stock
1 tablespoon cornstarch dissolved in ¼ cup
   sherry
1 tablespoon fresh chives
1 tablespoon fresh parsley, minced
1 tablespoon dried tarragon
1 tablespoon dried thyme
1 clove garlic, minced
¼ cup carrot, grated

T hicken stock by adding dissolved cornstarch and cooking
5 minutes until just boiling. Reduce heat, add herbs and garlic,
and simmer 2-3 minutes. Add grated carrot and simmer 1 minute more
until carrots are barely cooked.

◆

Nutritional Data

PER SERVING:		EXCHANGES:	
Calories:	38	Milk:	0.0
Fat (gm):	0.8	Vegetable:	0.2
Sat. fat (gm):	0.2	Fruit:	0.0
Cholesterol (mg):	0	Bread:	0.2
Sodium (mg):	394	Meat:	0.0
% Calories from fat:	20	Fat:	0.0

STUFFED PORK TENDERLOINS
with Sherry Herb Garden Sauce

Serves 6

3 extra-lean pork tenderloins, butterflied and
   lightly pounded
   Rice Stuffing (see recipe below)
   Toothpicks
2 cups *Sherry Herb Garden Sauce*

Rice Stuffing

2 cups cooked rice
½ cup tomato, chopped
½ cup green onions, sliced, tops included

Nutritional Data

PER SERVING:

Calories:	252
Fat (gm):	10.7
Sat. fat (gm):	3.8
Cholesterol (mg):	36.2
Sodium (mg):	292
% Calories from fat:	29

EXCHANGES:

Milk:	0.0	Bread:	1.2
Veg.:	0.4	Meat:	1.3
Fruit:	0.0	Fat:	1.3

Combine Rice Stuffing ingredients, and spread
stuffing evenly on pork tenderloins. Roll up jellyroll style and fasten with toothpicks. Roast in 350-degree oven 25-30 minutes until done. Cut each tenderloin in
half, and serve on Sherry Herb Garden Sauce.

POACHED COD FILLETS
with Sherry Herb Garden Sauce

Serves 6

1½ lbs. cod fillets
2 cups *Sherry Herb Garden Sauce*
3 tablespoons grated Parmesan cheese

Preheat oven to 350 degrees. Place cod in single
layer in casserole dish and pour sauce over fish.
Cover dish with foil and bring to boil atop stove.
Remove casserole to oven, and bake at 350 degrees
for 20 minutes.

Nutritional Data

PER SERVING:

Calories:	132
Fat (gm):	2.3
Sat. fat (gm):	0.9
Cholesterol (mg):	51.2
Sodium (mg):	383
% Calories from fat:	16

EXCHANGES:

Milk:	0.0	Bread:	0.1
Veg.:	0.1	Meat:	4.2
Fruit:	0.0	Fat:	0.1

ORANGE SAGE SAUCE

Yield 3 cups (6 half-cup servings)

2 cups defatted chicken stock, *or* beef stock
½ cup orange juice
1 tablespoon cornstarch dissolved in ¼ cup
   white wine or stock
1 tablespoon ground dried sage
1 orange, thinly sliced

ombine all ingredients except orange, and simmer 5 minutes over medium heat until gently bubbling. Cool, and stir in orange slices.

Nutritional Data

PER SERVING:		EXCHANGES:	
Calories:	44	Milk:	0.0
Fat (gm):	0.5	Vegetable:	0.0
Sat. fat (gm):	0.1	Fruit:	0.3
Cholesterol (mg):	0	Bread:	0.1
Sodium (mg):	259	Meat:	0.0
% Calories from fat:	11	Fat:	0.1

ORANGE GRILLED FLANK STEAK

Serves 6

1½ lbs. extra-lean flank steak, marinated
    (see recipe below)
2 cups *Orange Sage Sauce*

Marinade

1 cup orange juice
2 tablespoons red wine vinegar
1 clove garlic, crushed
    Zest of 1 orange

Combine Marinade ingredients, and marinate flank
steak at least 1 hour or overnight. Remove steak and
grill over hot coals or in very hot oven 3-5 minutes
per side. Slice thinly across the grain and serve with Orange Sage Sauce.

Nutritional Data

PER SERVING:

Calories:	296
Fat (gm):	12.1
Sat. fat (gm):	5.1
Cholesterol (mg):	76.3
Sodium (mg):	354
% Calories from fat:	30

EXCHANGES:

Milk:	0.0	Bread:	0.1
Veg.:	0.0	Meat:	4.3
Fruit:	0.7	Fat:	0.1

FLORIDA SUNSHINE CHICKEN

Serves 6

6 chicken legs, skin removed
2 tablespoons low-sodium soy sauce
6 orange slices
6 fresh sage leaves
2 cups *Orange Sage Sauce*

Combine chicken and soy sauce. Place in roasting
pan in single layer and top with orange slices. Place
a fresh sage leaf on each orange slice. Top off with
Orange Sage Sauce. Bake at 350 degrees for 45 minutes, basting often.

Nutritional Data

PER SERVING:

Calories:	121
Fat (gm):	2.7
Sat. fat (gm):	0.7
Cholesterol (mg):	47.7
Sodium (mg):	584
% Calories from fat:	20

EXCHANGES:

Milk:	0.0	Bread:	0.1
Veg.:	0.0	Meat:	1.3
Fruit:	0.3	Fat:	0.1

Orange Grilled Flank Steak

Serves 4

Florida Sunshine Chicken

Serves 6

5.
MEDITERRANEAN SAUCES AND MARINADES

♦

Italian Fennel Sauce

♦

Red Wine and Thyme Sauce

♦

White Wine/White Grape Sauce

♦

Balsamic Vinegar Sauce

♦

Greek Lemon Sauce

♦

Tomato, Caper, and Black Olive Sauce

♦

Italian Zucchini, Peppers, and Eggplant Sauce

♦

Garlic and Basil Sauce

ITALIAN FENNEL SAUCE

Yield 3 cups *(6 half-cup servings)*

2 cups clam juice, *or* fish stock
1 cup fennel bulb, sliced
1 tablespoon cornstarch dissolved in ½ cup
   white wine
¼ cup fennel tops, chopped
½ tablespoon fresh tarragon

Simmer fennel bulbs in clam juice 30 minutes. Thicken with cornstarch and wine mixture, and simmer 5 more minutes. Add fennel tops and fresh tarragon and stir well.

Nutritional Data

PER SERVING:		EXCHANGES:	
Calories:	83	Milk:	0.0
Fat (gm):	1.3	Vegetable:	0.0
Sat. fat (gm):	trace	Fruit:	0.6
Cholesterol (mg):	0	Bread:	0.1
Sodium (mg):	329	Meat:	0.0
% Calories from fat:	13	Fat:	0.3

BAKED POTATOES WITH PERNOD
in Italian Fennel Sauce

Serves 6

2½ cups potatoes, thinly sliced
  2 tablespoons Pernod liqueur
  2 cups *Italian Fennel Sauce*

Preheat oven to 350 degrees. Toss potato slices
gently in Pernod, coating on all sides. Place in
baking dish and cover with Fennel Sauce. Bake
30-45 minutes until potatoes are cooked through
and tender.

Nutritional Data

PER SERVING:

Calories:	185
Fat (gm):	2.2
Sat. fat (gm):	0.6
Cholesterol (mg):	0.8
Sodium (mg):	337
% Calories from fat:	11

EXCHANGES:

Milk:	0.0	Bread:	1.0
Veg.:	0.0	Meat:	0.0
Fruit:	0.7	Fat:	0.6

BAKED WHITE FISH
with Italian Fennel Sauce

Serves 6

1½ lbs. white fish fillets (such as cod or sole)
  1 clove garlic
  ¼ cup white wine
  3 cups *Italian Fennel Sauce*

Crush garlic and rub open end over fish fillets. Place
fish in baking dish and cover with wine. Bake at 350
degrees 20-25 minutes. When cooked, spoon Italian
Fennel Sauce over fillets.

Nutritional Data

PER SERVING:

Calories:	183
Fat (gm):	2
Sat. fat (gm):	0.2
Cholesterol (mg):	48.7
Sodium (mg):	391
% Calories from fat:	10

EXCHANGES:

Milk:	0.0	Bread:	0.1
Veg.:	0.0	Meat:	4.0
Fruit:	0.6	Fat:	0.4

RED WINE AND THYME SAUCE

Yield 3 cups *(6 half-cup servings)*

 2 cups defatted beef stock
 1 cup red wine
 ¼ cup onion, minced
 ¼ cup fresh parsley, minced
 ½ tablespoon cornstarch dissolved in ¼ cup
    water
 ¼ cup fresh thyme

Bring stock, wine, onion, and parsley to a rolling boil. Reduce heat and simmer 5 minutes. Thicken with cornstarch and water mixture, stirring constantly. Add fresh thyme.

Nutritional Data

PER SERVING:		EXCHANGES:	
Calories:	43	Milk:	0.0
Fat (gm):	0.3	Vegetable:	0.1
Sat. fat (gm):	0.1	Fruit:	0.0
Cholesterol (mg):	0	Bread:	0.1
Sodium (mg):	265	Meat:	0.0
% Calories from fat:	6	Fat:	0.6

STUFFED BEEF TENDERLOINS
with Red Wine and Thyme Sauce

Serves 6

6 fillets cut from tenderloin
  Vegetable Stuffing (see recipe below)
½ tablespoon canola oil
3 cups *Red Wine and Thyme Sauce*

Vegetable Stuffing

1 cup carrots, finely diced
1 cup celery, finely diced
1 cup onion, finely diced
1 tablespoon canola oil
1 tablespoon water
¼ cup breadcrumbs
1 tablespoon dried thyme

Nutritional Data

PER SERVING:

Calories:	282
Fat (gm):	10.2
Sat. fat (gm):	1.7
Cholesterol (mg):	65.5
Sodium (mg):	375
% Calories from fat:	30

EXCHANGES:

Milk:	0.0	Bread:	0.3
Veg.:	0.8	Meat:	0.3
Fruit:	0.0	Fat:	1.9

First prepare Vegetable Stuffing by sautéeing vegetables in oil until they sizzle. Then turn heat down to low, and continue steaming vegetables until tender, adding water if necessary. Mix in breadcrumbs and thyme, and set stuffing aside.

Coat another skillet with oil, and heat until just smoking. Brown fillets on all sides and place on baking sheet. Cut slit in side of each steak and spoon in Vegetable Stuffing. Finish cooking in 400-degree oven 8 more minutes for medium-rare meat. Serve accompanied by Red Wine and Thyme Sauce.

PEAS, MUSHROOMS, AND PEARL ONIONS
in Red Wine and Thyme Sauce

Serves 6

2 cups *Red Wine and Thyme Sauce*
2 cups frozen pearl onions
2 tablespoons canola oil
1 lb. fresh mushrooms
2 cups frozen peas
  Salt and pepper to taste

Nutritional Data

PER SERVING:

Calories:	160
Fat (gm):	5.5
Sat. fat (gm):	1.4
Cholesterol (mg):	0
Sodium (mg):	539
% Calories from fat:	29

EXCHANGES:

Milk:	0.0	Bread:	0.5
Veg.:	1.7	Meat:	0.0
Fruit:	0.0	Fat:	1.4

Bring Red Wine and Thyme Sauce to boil. Add pearl onions and simmer until tender.

In non-stick skillet brushed with oil, sauté mushrooms. Lightly salt, cover pan, and turn heat to low for 10 minutes. Remove lid and turn heat to high to evaporate liquid.

When most of liquid is evaporated, add peas, onions, and Red Wine and Thyme Sauce. Season with salt and pepper. Heat thoroughly before serving.

WHITE WINE/WHITE GRAPE SAUCE

♦

Yield 3 cups (12 quarter-cup servings)

2 cups defatted chicken stock, *or* fish stock
½ cup sauterne, or other sweet white wine
¼ cup onion, minced
1 large clove garlic, minced
2 tablespoons cornstarch dissolved in ¼ cup stock
¼ cup fresh parsley, minced
1 cup white seedless grapes
¼ cup almonds, sliced

C ombine first 4 ingredients and bring to rolling boil. Reduce heat and simmer 15 minutes. Thicken with cornstarch and stock mixture and cook, stirring constantly, 2 minutes. Add parsley and grapes and heat thoroughly. Garnish with sliced almonds.

♦

Nutritional Data

PER SERVING:		EXCHANGES:	
Calories:	46	Milk:	0.0
Fat (gm):	1.8	Vegetable:	0.5
Sat. fat (gm):	0.2	Fruit:	0.2
Cholesterol (mg):	0	Bread:	0.1
Sodium (mg):	131	Meat:	0.1
% Calories from fat:	17	Fat:	0.4

GRILLED TURKEY MEDALLIONS
with White Wine/White Grape Sauce

Serves 6

1½ lbs. turkey medallions, marinated (see recipe below)

3 cups *White Wine/White Grape Sauce*

Marinade

1 clove garlic

¼ cup red onion, minced

¼ cup white wine

2 tablespoons white wine vinegar

2 tablespoons honey

Nutritional Data

PER SERVING:

Calories:	282
Fat (gm):	4.9
Sat. fat (gm):	0.9
Cholesterol (mg):	97.2
Sodium (mg):	326
% Calories from fat:	16

EXCHANGES:

Milk:	0.0	Bread:	0.2
Veg.:	0.2	Meat:	3.0
Fruit:	0.7	Fat:	0.9

Combine Marinade ingredients, and marinate turkey medallions 1 hour. Because medallions will cook quickly, grill them over hot coals or broil them in hot broiler approximately 2-3 minutes per side or until no longer pink. Serve topped with White Wine/White Grape Sauce.

FILLET OF SOLE
with White Wine/White Grape Sauce

Serves 6

1½ lbs. sole fillets (or other mild, white fish)

3 cups *White Wine/White Grape Sauce*

Lemon slices for garnish

Preheat oven to 350 degrees. Lay fish flat in baking dish, and ladle sauce generously over fillets. Cover dish with foil and bake 25 minutes. Garnish with fresh lemon slices.

Nutritional Data

PER SERVING:

Calories:	195
Fat (gm):	4.9
Sat. fat (gm):	0.8
Cholesterol (mg):	54.4
Sodium (mg):	353
% Calories from fat:	23

EXCHANGES:

Milk:	0.0	Bread:	0.2
Veg.:	0.1	Meat:	4.1
Fruit:	0.4	Fat:	0.7

BALSAMIC VINEGAR SAUCE

Yield 3 cups *(6 half-cup servings)*

2 cups defatted chicken stock
¼ cup minced shallots
1 tablespoon cornstarch dissolved in ¼ cup water
2 tablespoons balsamic vinegar
2 tablespoons sugar
  Salt and pepper to taste

Bring stock and shallots to boil. Reduce heat and simmer 5 minutes. Thicken with cornstarch and water mixture. Add vinegar and sugar, and simmer 5 minutes to combine flavors. Season with salt and pepper.

Nutritional Data

PER SERVING:		EXCHANGES:	
Calories:	40	Milk:	0.0
Fat (gm):	0.5	Vegetable:	0.2
Sat. fat (gm):	0.3	Fruit:	0.3
Cholesterol (mg):	0	Bread:	0.1
Sodium (mg):	260	Meat:	0.0
% Calories from fat:	11	Fat:	0.0

RED POTATOES, GREEN BEANS, AND MUSHROOMS
with Balsamic Vinegar Sauce

Serves 6

1 lb. red potatoes

2 cups French-style green beans, frozen

3 cups *Balsamic Vinegar Sauce*

½ lb. fresh mushrooms, sliced

Cut potatoes and beans into bite-size pieces. Bring sauce to boil. Add potatoes and cook 15 minutes. Add green beans and cook 5 more minutes, until thoroughly cooked.

Add mushrooms and cook another 5 minutes until all vegetables are crisp but not overcooked. Drain and reserve sauce for serving and presentation.

Nutritional Data

PER SERVING:

Calories:	131
Fat (gm):	0.8
Sat. fat (gm):	0.2
Cholesterol (mg):	0
Sodium (mg):	267
% Calories from fat:	5

EXCHANGES:

Milk:	0.0	Bread:	1.1
Veg.:	0.9	Meat:	0.0
Fruit:	0.3	Fat:	0.0

TUNA AND RED ONIONS
with Balsamic Vinegar Sauce

Serves 6

¼ cup honey

¼ cup balsamic vinegar

1 large red onion, thinly sliced into rings

6 tuna, *or* swordfish steaks

3 cups *Balsamic Vinegar Sauce*

Dissolve honey in balsamic vinegar. Marinate onion in this mixture 30 minutes. Place fish steaks in baking dish. Evenly distribute onions and marinade over fish steaks. Pour Balsamic Vinegar Sauce over all, and bake in 350-degree oven 15-20 minutes. Fish steaks should be served slightly pink in center.

Nutritional Data

PER SERVING:

Calories:	113
Fat (gm):	1.3
Sat. fat (gm):	0.3
Cholesterol (mg):	6.1
Sodium (mg):	267
% Calories from fat:	10

EXCHANGES:

Milk:	0.0	Bread:	0.1
Veg.:	0.5	Meat:	0.6
Fruit:	1.0	Fat:	0.0

GREEK LEMON SAUCE

Yield 2 cups (4 half-cup servings)

2 cups defatted chicken stock
1 clove garlic, minced
½ teaspoon dried oregano
2 tablespoons shallots, minced
Juice and zest of 1 lemon
Salt and pepper to taste

Combine first 4 ingredients. Bring to boil, then reduce heat and simmer 5 minutes. Add lemon juice and zest. Season with salt and pepper.

Nutritional Data

PER SERVING:		EXCHANGES:	
Calories:	29	Milk:	0.0
Fat (gm):	0.8	Vegetable:	0.2
Sat. fat (gm):	0.2	Fruit:	0.2
Cholesterol (mg):	0	Bread:	0.0
Sodium (mg):	389	Meat:	0.0
% Calories from fat:	23	Fat:	0.0

WILTED SPINACH SALAD
with Turkey Bacon, Shrimp, and Greek Lemon Sauce

Serves 6

3 slices turkey bacon, *or* vegetarian bacon
1 lb. cooked shrimp, peeled, deveined
2 cups *Greek Lemon Sauce*
2 tablespoons red wine vinegar
1 lb. fresh spinach, cleaned, dried
¼ red onion, sliced into thin rings
2 medium tomatoes, finely diced

In skillet, brown bacon, draining well. Add shrimp, Greek Lemon Sauce, and vinegar. Heat thoroughly and pour over spinach leaves to wilt. Garnish salad with red onion slices and diced tomatoes.

Nutritional Data

PER SERVING:

Calories:	121
Fat (gm):	3.3
Sat. fat (gm):	0.6
Cholesterol (mg):	99.3
Sodium (mg):	509
% Calories from fat:	24

EXCHANGES:

Milk:	0.0	Bread:	0.0
Veg.:	0.9	Meat:	2.3
Fruit:	0.1	Fat:	0.3

GREEK CHICKEN AND RICE

Serves 8

¼ cup raisins
¼ cup almonds, sliced
¼ cup onion, diced
1 cup uncooked long-grain rice
2 large cloves garlic, minced
1 tablespoon fresh oregano
1 tablespoon fresh basil
1 tablespoon thyme
1 lemon, sliced
1 qt. defatted chicken stock
3½ lbs. chicken pieces
2 cups *Greek Lemon Sauce*

Nutritional Data

PER SERVING:

Calories:	316
Fat (gm):	8.5
Sat. fat (gm):	1.4
Cholesterol (mg):	100
Sodium (mg):	8
% Calories from fat:	19

EXCHANGES:

Milk:	0.0	Bread:	0.8
Veg.:	0.2	Meat:	5.0
Fruit:	0.4	Fat:	1.0

Bring all ingredients, except chicken and Greek Lemon Sauce to a boil in oven-proof casserole. Top with chicken pieces, cover, and bake 1 hour in 350-degree oven. Add additional water if too much liquid evaporates.

Turn oven up to 425 degrees, uncover casserole dish, and bake another 10 minutes before serving with Greek Lemon Sauce.

TOMATO, CAPER, AND BLACK OLIVE SAUCE

Yield 2 cups *(8 quarter-cup servings)*

2 tablespoons olive oil
1 large clove garlic
1 10-oz. can of tomatoes
2 tablespoons low-sodium tomato paste
½ cup capers
½ cup black olives, sliced
1 tablespoon fresh basil
1 tablespoon sugar

auté garlic in oil. Add tomatoes and simmer 15 minutes. Add all remaining ingredients and heat thoroughly.

Nutritional Data

PER SERVING:		EXCHANGES:	
Calories:	69	Milk:	0.0
Fat (gm):	5	Vegetable:	0.5
Sat. fat (gm):	0.7	Fruit:	0.1
Cholesterol (mg):	0	Bread:	0.0
Sodium (mg):	156	Meat:	0.0
% Calories from fat:	14	Fat:	1.0

VEAL SHANKS AND PASTA
with Tomato, Caper, and Black Olive Sauce

Serves 6

6 veal shanks (preferably hind shanks)
2 tablespoons canola oil
1 onion, roughly chopped
2 carrots, roughly chopped
1 celery stalk, roughly chopped
1 tablespoon fresh thyme
1 bay leaf
1½ cups defatted chicken stock
2 cups *Tomato, Caper, and Black Olive Sauce*
6 cups cooked pasta (any kind)

Nutritional Data

PER SERVING:

Calories:	348
Fat (gm):	12.9
Sat. fat (gm):	4.1
Cholesterol (mg):	56.6
Sodium (mg):	289
% Calories from fat:	31

EXCHANGES:

Milk:	0.0	Bread:	1.5
Veg.:	0.8	Meat:	2.0
Fruit:	0.1	Fat:	1.9

Heat oil in pan until just smoking, and brown shanks on all sides. Move shanks to large Dutch oven, and cover with vegetables, herbs, and stock. Bring to boil, cover pot, and place in oven. Bake at 350 degrees about 2 hours. Serve shanks with Tomato, Caper, and Black Olive Sauce over pasta.

BAKED COD IN WINE
with Tomato, Caper, and Black Olive Sauce

Serves 6

1½ lbs. cod fillets, *or* other mild, white fish
1 tablespoon fresh basil
1 clove garlic, minced
1 cup calorie-reduced white wine
2 cups *Tomato, Caper, and Black Olive Sauce*

Nutritional Data

PER SERVING:

Calories:	196
Fat (gm):	7.5
Sat. fat (gm):	1
Cholesterol (mg):	48.7
Sodium (mg):	271
% Calories from fat:	30

EXCHANGES:

Milk:	0.0	Bread:	0.0
Veg.:	0.6	Meat:	4.0
Fruit:	0.1	Fat:	1.7

Preheat oven to 325 degrees. Place cod fillets in baking dish. Evenly coat with basil and garlic. Pour wine over fish, and cover dish with aluminum foil. Bake at 325 degrees 25 minutes or until done. Serve atop Tomato, Caper, and Black Olive Sauce.

ITALIAN ZUCCHINI, PEPPERS, AND EGGPLANT SAUCE

Yield 3 cups (6 half-cup servings)

1 medium yellow onion
1 medium eggplant
2 small zucchini
2 small yellow squash
1 red bell pepper
1 green bell pepper
1 tablespoon salt
3 tablespoons olive oil
1 large clove garlic
1 10-oz. can tomatoes
1 tablespoon fresh basil

K eeping vegetables separate, slice onion, cut eggplant into 1-inch cubes (skin included), and cut zucchini and squash into thick pieces. Cut peppers into strips.

In separate colanders, toss eggplant and zucchini with salt. Let drain at least ½ hour. Rinse thoroughly to remove salt.

Heat olive oil in skillet, and sauté vegetables separately, keeping them undercooked. When all vegetables are sautéed, combine them with all remaining ingredients and simmer 30 minutes.

Nutritional Data

PER SERVING:		EXCHANGES:	
Calories:	100	Milk:	0.0
Fat (gm):	8.7	Vegetable:	2.5
Sat. fat (gm):	1.3	Fruit:	0.0
Cholesterol (mg):	0	Bread:	0.0
Sodium (mg):	87	Meat:	0.0
% Calories from fat:	26	Fat:	1.5

LAMB AND RED ONION SKEWERS
with Italian Zucchini, Peppers, and Eggplant Sauce

Serves 6 *(2 skewers per serving)*

- 3 lbs. leg of lamb, boned, cut into 1½-inch cubes
- 1 large red onion, quartered, layers separated
- 12 wooden skewers, presoaked in cold water 20 minutes
- 1 tablespoon dried oregano
- 2 tablespoons olive oil
- 3 cups *Italian Zucchini, Peppers, and Eggplant Sauce*

Nutritional Data

PER SERVING:

Calories:	307
Fat (gm):	15.8
Sat. fat (gm):	4.1
Cholesterol (mg):	101
Sodium (mg):	121
% Calories from fat:	30

EXCHANGES:

Milk:	0.0	Bread:	0.0
Veg.:	1.4	Meat:	4.0
Fruit:	0.0	Fat:	1.3

Assemble skewers, alternating lamb cubes and onion. Brush with olive oil and sprinkle with oregano. Grill over hot coals or broil in oven until medium-rare. Serve with Italian Zucchini, Peppers, and Eggplant Sauce for dipping.

VEGETARIAN PIZZA
with Italian Zucchini, Peppers, and Eggplant Sauce

Serves 8

Pizza Dough

- 2 tablespoons honey
- 1 cup warm water
- 1 tablespoon dry yeast
- 2 tablespoons olive oil
- 1 teaspoon salt
- ¼ teaspoon dried oregano
- 3 cups white flour

Pizza Topping

Nutritional Data

PER SERVING:

Calories:	346
Fat (gm):	12
Sat. fat (gm):	2.2
Cholesterol (mg):	2.7
Sodium (mg):	229
% Calories from fat:	31

EXCHANGES:

Milk:	0.0	Bread:	2.1
Veg.:	2.0	Meat:	0.5
Fruit:	0.3	Fat:	2.0

- 2 cups *Italian Zucchini, Peppers, and Eggplant Sauce*
- 1 cup low-fat mozzarella cheese, shredded

To make Pizza Dough, dissolve honey in water. Add yeast and wait 5 minutes until bubbly. Add olive oil, salt, and oregano. Begin stirring in flour until it's completely absorbed.

Knead for several minutes on floured surface. Let dough rise 15-20 minutes in covered bowl. Shape into pizza shell, and top with Italian Zucchini, Peppers, and Eggplant Sauce and mozzarella. Bake at 450 degrees 8 minutes or until slightly browned.

GARLIC AND BASIL SAUCE

Yield 3 cups *(6 half-cup servings)*

2 cups defatted chicken stock
2 large cloves garlic, minced
1 tomato, peeled, seeds removed
¼ cup shallots, minced
1 tablespoon cornstarch dissolved in ¼ cup
   white wine
½ cup fresh basil leaves, chopped
   Salt and pepper to taste

Bring stock, garlic, tomato, and shallots to boil. Stir mixture to blend in tomato pulp thoroughly. Reduce heat and simmer 15 minutes. Thicken with cornstarch and white wine mixture, and simmer 5 more minutes. Add basil leaves. Season with salt and pepper.

Nutritional Data

PER SERVING:		EXCHANGES:	
Calories:	30	Milk:	0.0
Fat (gm):	0.6	Vegetable:	0.4
Sat. fat (gm):	0.1	Fruit:	0.0
Cholesterol (mg):	0	Bread:	0.1
Sodium (mg):	262	Meat:	0.0
% Calories from fat:	17	Fat:	0.0

BRAISED SWORDFISH PEPPER STEAKS
with Garlic and Basil Sauce

Serves 6

6 swordfish steaks cut 1 inch thick
3 tablespoons olive oil, divided
¼ cup freshly cracked black pepper
3 cups *Garlic and Basil Sauce*

Preheat oven to 350 degrees. Brush steaks liberally
with half the olive oil, and sprinkle both sides with
pepper. Sear swordfish steaks in very hot non-stick
skillet. Brush with olive oil again. Place seared
steaks in baking dish, and cover with Garlic and
Basil Sauce. Cook 10-15 minutes in 350-degree oven
until sauce is bubbly.

Nutritional Data

PER SERVING:

Calories:	283
Fat (gm):	16.1
Sat. fat (gm):	3.5
Cholesterol (mg):	53
Sodium (mg):	386
% Calories from fat:	28

EXCHANGES:

Milk:	0.0	Bread:	0.1
Veg.:	0.4	Meat:	4.8
Fruit:	0.0	Fat:	2.6

TUNA SKEWER AND BOW TIE PASTA
with Garlic and Basil Sauce

Serves 6

1 lb. tuna cut into 1-inch cubes
1 red bell pepper cut into 1-inch pieces
1 green bell pepper cut into 1-inch pieces
1 zucchini cut into 1-inch pieces
½ lb. mushrooms
6 bamboo skewers, soaked in cold water
   30 minutes
1 clove garlic, crushed
3 cups *Garlic and Basil Sauce*
4 cups cooked bow tie pasta

Nutritional Data

PER SERVING:

Calories:	299
Fat (gm):	5.3
Sat. fat (gm):	1.2
Cholesterol (mg):	28.7
Sodium (mg):	297
% Calories from fat:	16

EXCHANGES:

Milk:	0.0	Bread:	1.8
Veg.:	1.6	Meat:	2.6
Fruit:	0.0	Fat:	0.0

Assemble skewers alternating fish and vegetables. After assembling, rub each
completed skewer with crushed garlic clove. Then coat each skewer with Garlic
and Basil Sauce.

Grill or broil until fish is thoroughly cooked, about 3-4 minutes, turning
halfway through. Toss bow tie pasta with remaining sauce. Serve 1 skewer to each
person atop pasta.

WHITE BEAN AND CHICKEN RAGOUT
with Garlic and Basil Sauce

Serves 6

- 3 cups cooked white beans
- 3 cups grilled chicken meat, skin removed, cubed
- 3 cups *Garlic and Basil Sauce*
- 1 cup breadcrumbs
- 1/4 cup Parmesan cheese, grated

Preheat oven to 350 degrees. Combine beans, chicken, and sauce in casserole dish. Top with breadcrumbs and Parmesan cheese. Bake 30-45 minutes at 350 degrees until casserole is bubbly and top is browned.

Nutritional Data

PER SERVING:

Calories:	321
Fat (gm):	7.3
Sat. fat (gm):	1.5
Cholesterol (mg):	100
Sodium (mg):	646
% Calories from fat:	18

EXCHANGES:

Milk:	0.0	Bread:	2.2
Veg.:	0.4	Meat:	4.2
Fruit:	0.0	Fat:	0.3

6.
ASIAN SAUCES
AND MARINADES

Sherry, Ginger, and Garlic Sauce

Peach Sweet-and-Sour Sauce

Light Thai Peanut Sauce

Lemon Sesame Sauce

Lemon-Basil-Mint Sauce

Sherry, Ginger, and Garlic Sauce

Yield 3 cups (6 half-cup servings)

1 tablespoon ginger root, freshly grated
1 large clove garlic, minced
2 tablespoons sherry
1¾ tablespoons low-sodium soy sauce
1 tablespoon sugar
1 tablespoon honey
2½ cups defatted chicken stock
2 tablespoons cornstarch dissolved in ½ cup defatted chicken stock

C ombine first 7 ingredients and bring to rolling boil. Lower heat and simmer 10 minutes until garlic and ginger are cooked. Add cornstarch and stock mixture, and stir constantly until thickened.

Nutritional Data

PER SERVING:		EXCHANGES:	
Calories:	54	Milk:	0.0
Fat (gm):	0.6	Vegetable:	0.0
Sat. fat (gm):	0.2	Fruit:	0.3
Cholesterol (mg):	0	Bread:	0.2
Sodium (mg):	595	Meat:	0.0
% Calories from fat:	10	Fat:	0.1

STEAK WITH SWEET PEPPERS
and Sherry, Ginger, and Garlic Sauce

Serves 6

1½ lbs. flank, *or* sirloin steak, cut into ½-inch-wide strips

1¾ tablespoons peanut oil, divided

1 red bell pepper, cut into ½-inch strips

1 green bell pepper, cut into ½-inch strips

1 yellow or purple bell pepper, cut into ½-inch strips

2 cups *Sherry, Ginger, and Garlic Sauce*

Nutritional Data

PER SERVING:

Calories:	242
Fat (gm):	11.5
Sat. fat (gm):	4
Cholesterol (mg):	57.2
Sodium (mg):	527
% Calories from fat:	30

EXCHANGES:

Milk:	0.0	Bread:	0.1
Veg.:	0.4	Meat:	3.2
Fruit:	0.2	Fat:	0.5

Brush wok or skillet with 1 tablespoon peanut oil and bring to high heat. Stir-fry bell pepper strips 5-6 minutes until tender but still crisp. Remove and reserve.

Brush wok or skillet with remaining oil and heat again. Stir-fry beef strips, then add pepper strips and Sherry, Ginger, and Garlic Sauce for an additional 3 minutes to combine flavors. Serve hot, with or without rice.

CASHEW CHICKEN
with Sherry, Ginger, and Garlic Sauce

Serves 8

½ lb. chicken, skinless, cubed

4 tablespoons peanut oil

½ lb. well-drained, firm tofu, cubed

¼ cup frozen peas

¼ cup canned water chestnuts, sliced

¼ cup carrots, sliced

¼ cup green onions, sliced

1 cup (total) red and green bell pepper strips

3 cups *Sherry, Ginger, and Garlic Sauce*

1 cup cashews, chopped

Nutritional Data

PER SERVING:

Calories:	263
Fat (gm):	16.9
Sat. fat (gm):	3.1
Cholesterol (mg):	16.4
Sodium (mg):	485
% Calories from fat:	26

EXCHANGES:

Milk:	0.0	Bread:	0.2
Veg.:	0.4	Meat:	1.2
Fruit:	0.2	Fat:	2.5

In wok or skillet brushed with peanut oil, stir-fry chicken 4-5 minutes and reserve. Stir-fry tofu 3-4 minutes and reserve. Combine vegetables and stir-fry until just crisp.

Add chicken and tofu to wok and heat to sizzling. Add Sherry, Ginger, and Garlic Sauce. Serve topped with cashews, with or without rice.

PEACH SWEET-AND-SOUR SAUCE

Yield 3 cups *(12 quarter-cup servings)*

2   cups reduced-sugar peach preserves
1   large clove garlic, minced
¼   cup ketchup
¼   cup red wine vinegar
1   tablespoon Worcestershire sauce
2   tablespoons low-sodium soy sauce

 ombine all ingredients and bring to boil. Reduce heat and simmer 5 minutes.

Nutritional Data

PER SERVING:		EXCHANGES:	
Calories:	86	Milk:	0.0
Fat (gm):	0.1	Vegetable:	0.5
Sat. fat (gm):	trace	Fruit:	1.4
Cholesterol (mg):	0	Bread:	0.0
Sodium (mg):	219	Meat:	0.0
% Calories from fat:	1	Fat:	0.0

SMOKED PORK CHOPS
with Peach Sweet-and-Sour Sauce

Serves 6
6 medium-size smoked pork chops
2½ cups *Peach Sweet-and-Sour Sauce*

Brown chops in heavy cast-iron skillet over high heat. After all sides are thoroughly browned, pour in Peach Sweet-and-Sour Sauce. Bring to boil, then reduce heat and simmer 15-20 minutes. Add a table-spoon or two of water if sauce becomes too thick and sticky. Serve with or without rice.

Nutritional Data
PER SERVING:

Calories:	320
Fat (gm):	15
Sat. fat (gm):	3.5
Cholesterol (mg):	81.8
Sodium (mg):	483
% Calories from fat:	30

EXCHANGES:

Milk:	0.0	Bread:	0.0
Veg.:	0.1	Meat:	3.0
Fruit:	2.5	Fat:	1.3

PEACH SWEET-AND-SOUR SHRIMP

Serves 6
2 tablespoons peanut oil
1 cup red bell pepper strips
1 cup frozen snow peas
1 lb. fresh shrimp, cleaned and deveined
¼ cup canned water chestnut slices
3 cups *Peach Sweet-and-Sour Sauce*

Stir-fry pepper strips and snow peas separately in wok or skillet brushed with oil. Vegetables should be barely cooked and still crisp. Remove from wok and reserve.

Nutritional Data
PER SERVING:

Calories:	317
Fat (gm):	6.1
Sat. fat (gm):	1
Cholesterol (mg):	115
Sodium (mg):	551
% Calories from fat:	17

EXCHANGES:

Milk:	0.0	Bread:	0.0
Veg.:	1.2	Meat:	2.3
Fruit:	2.8	Fat:	0.9

Stir-fry shrimp until they turn pink and curl slightly. Return snow peas and pepper slices to wok; add water chestnuts. When this combination is sizzling, add Peach Sweet-and-Sour Sauce and bring to boil. Serve with or without rice or noodles.

LIGHT THAI PEANUT SAUCE

Yield 3 cups *(12 quarter-cup servings)*

1 cup defatted chicken stock
½ cup chunky-style, low-fat, low-sodium peanut
    butter
1 clove garlic
1 cup carrot, shredded
2 tablespoons rice wine vinegar, *or* other white
    vinegar
1 tablespoon sugar
1 tablespoon hot pepper flakes

ombine all ingredients and heat thoroughly, stirring to completely incorporate peanut butter. Do not boil.

Nutritional Data

PER SERVING:		EXCHANGES:	
Calories:	99	Milk:	0.0
Fat (gm):	9.7	Vegetable:	0.3
Sat. fat (gm):	2.1	Fruit:	0.6
Cholesterol (mg):	0	Bread:	0.0
Sodium (mg):	72	Meat:	1.3
% Calories from fat:	29	Fat:	1.5

MINI TURKEY BURGERS
with Light Thai Peanut Sauce

Serves 10

1½ lbs. ground turkey, extra lean
1 tablespoon low-sodium soy sauce
¼ cup onion, minced
2 tablespoons ketchup
1 egg white
1¾ tablespoons peanut oil
3 cups *Light Thai Peanut Sauce*

Combine all ingredients, except oil and Light Thai
Peanut Sauce, and chill 30 minutes. Form into 10
small patties. Grill or broil in non-stick skillet
brushed with oil. Cook thoroughly and serve on dollar-size buns with Light Thai
Peanut Sauce.

Nutritional Data
PER SERVING:

Calories:	341
Fat (gm):	23.5
Sat. fat (gm):	3.3
Cholesterol (mg):	69.4
Sodium (mg):	245
% Calories from fat:	30

EXCHANGES:

Milk:	0.0	Bread:	0.0
Veg.:	0.2	Meat:	3.7
Fruit:	0.4	Fat:	1.9

CURRIED PORK APPETIZER SKEWERS
with Light Thai Peanut Sauce

Serves 10

1½ cups small, lean pork cubes, cut from loin
   or shoulder, marinated (see recipe below)
1 cup green bell pepper, cut into 1-inch cubes
1 cup onion, cut into 1-inch cubes
10 wooden skewers, presoaked in cold water
   20 minutes
3 cups *Light Thai Peanut Sauce*

Marinade

¼ cup honey
¼ cup white wine
2 tablespoons curry powder

Combine Marinade ingredients and marinate pork at least 1 hour in refrigerator.
Thread pork and vegetables on skewers, and broil or grill over medium heat,
basting often with Marinade, 20-25 minutes. Serve with Light Thai Peanut Sauce
as accompaniment.

Nutritional Data
PER SERVING:

Calories:	299
Fat (gm):	17.9
Sat. fat (gm):	4.2
Cholesterol (mg):	35.8
Sodium (mg):	113
% Calories from fat:	30

EXCHANGES:

Milk:	0.0	Bread:	0.0
Veg.:	0.6	Meat:	2.0
Fruit:	0.8	Fat:	2.1

LEMON SESAME SAUCE

Yield 3 cups *(12 quarter-cup servings)*

2 cups defatted chicken stock
1 clove garlic, minced
1 tablespoon fresh ginger, minced
1 tablespoon cornstarch dissolved in ¼ cup rice
   wine vinegar, *or* other white vinegar
2 tablespoons lemon juice
1¼ cups sesame seeds, toasted in dry skillet until
   browned

Combine stock, garlic, ginger and simmer over medium heat 5 minutes. Thicken with cornstarch and vinegar mixture, stirring constantly. Add juice and toasted sesame seeds.

Nutritional Data

PER SERVING:		EXCHANGES:	
Calories:	97	Milk:	0.0
Fat (gm):	7.8	Vegetable:	0.0
Sat. fat (gm):	1.1	Fruit:	0.0
Cholesterol (mg):	0	Bread:	0.5
Sodium (mg):	131	Meat:	0.0
% Calories from fat:	15	Fat:	1.7

ASPARAGUS CHICKEN
with Lemon Sesame Sauce

Serves 6

3 boneless chicken breasts, skin removed
1⅓ lbs. asparagus, cleaned and trimmed
3 cups *Lemon Sesame Sauce*

Cut asparagus into equal lengths and blanch in boiling water until tender but still crisp. Bring Lemon Sesame Sauce to boil. Add chicken and simmer until cooked, approximately 6-7 minutes or until meat is no longer pink. Serve over hot asparagus.

Nutritional Data

PER SERVING:

Calories:	281
Fat (gm):	16.3
Sat. fat (gm):	2.5
Cholesterol (mg):	34.2
Sodium (mg):	303
% Calories from fat:	30

EXCHANGES:

Milk:	0.0	Bread:	0.1
Veg.:	1.0	Meat:	1.5
Fruit:	0.0	Fat:	3.3

SESAME BAKED CHICKEN

Serves 6

6 boneless chicken breasts, skin removed
2 tablespoons Worcestershire sauce
¼ tablespoon honey
2 tablespoons white wine
4 tablespoons sesame seeds
3 cups *Lemon Sesame Sauce*

Place chicken in baking dish. Combine Worcestershire, honey, and white wine and pour mixture onto chicken breasts. Sprinkle with sesame seeds. Bake at 375 degrees about 30 minutes. Serve with Lemon Sesame Sauce.

Nutritional Data

PER SERVING:

Calories:	343
Fat (gm):	20.3
Sat. fat (gm):	3.1
Cholesterol (mg):	68.4
Sodium (mg):	398
% Calories from fat:	30

EXCHANGES:

Milk:	0.0	Bread:	0.1
Veg.:	0.0	Meat:	3.0
Fruit:	0.3	Fat:	3.8

LEMON-BASIL-MINT SAUCE

Yield 3 cups (6 half-cup servings)

2 cups defatted chicken stock
1 large clove garlic, minced
1 tablespoon cornstarch dissolved in ¼ cup sherry
¼ cup fresh mint, minced
¼ cup fresh basil, minced
Juice and zest of 1 lemon

Bring stock and garlic to boil. Reduce heat and simmer 5 minutes. Add cornstarch and sherry mixture, stirring constantly. Add mint, basil, and lemon. Simmer 1 minute to combine flavors.

Nutritional Data

PER SERVING:		EXCHANGES:	
Calories:	22	Milk:	0.0
Fat (gm):	0.5	Vegetable:	0.0
Sat. fat (gm):	0.1	Fruit:	0.1
Cholesterol (mg):	0	Bread:	0.1
Sodium (mg):	259	Meat:	0.0
% Calories from fat:	20	Fat:	0.0

LEMON-BASIL-MINT CHICKEN

Serves 6

1 qt. water
½ cup carrots, diced
½ cup celery, diced
1 small head broccoli, diced
1 qt. ice water
2 cups *Lemon-Basil-Mint Sauce*
1½ lbs. boneless chicken breasts, skin removed, cut into 1-inch cubes
4 cups cooked pasta
¼ cup Parmesan cheese, grated

Nutritional Data

PER SERVING:

Calories:	303
Fat (gm):	3.8
Sat. fat (gm):	1.4
Cholesterol (mg):	69
Sodium (mg):	424
% Calories from fat:	12

EXCHANGES:

Milk:	0.0	Bread:	1.8
Veg.:	2.0	Meat:	3.1
Fruit:	0.1	Fat:	0.1

Boil water and blanch carrots, celery, and broccoli by immersing for 1 minute each. Upon removing from boiling water, plunge each vegetable into ice water. Bring Lemon-Basil-Mint Sauce to boil and add chicken cubes. Simmer 5 minutes or until chicken is cooked. Add vegetables and heat thoroughly. Serve over cooked pasta, and top with Parmesan cheese.

BAKED TILAPIA
with Lemon-Basil-Mint Sauce

Serves 6

1½ lbs. tilapia fillets (*or* catfish *or* cod)
1 clove garlic, minced
½ tablespoon fresh basil
½ tablespoon mint
Juice of 1 lemon
¼ cup white wine
2 cups *Lemon-Basil-Mint Sauce*

Nutritional Data

PER SERVING:

Calories:	135
Fat (gm):	1.9
Sat. fat (gm):	0.5
Cholesterol (mg):	54.4
Sodium (mg):	352
% Calories from fat:	13

EXCHANGES:

Milk:	0.0	Bread:	0.1
Veg.:	0.0	Meat:	4.0
Fruit:	0.2	Fat:	0.1

Place fillets in baking dish. Combine garlic, basil, mint, lemon, and white wine. Pour over fish, cover with foil, and bake at 350 degrees for 25 minutes. Serve with Lemon-Basil-Mint Sauce.

7.
CARIBBEAN AND TROPICAL SAUCES

Tomato-Orange Sauce

Island Rum-Lime Sauce

Spicy Mango Sauce

Papaya Ginger Sauce

Jamaican Jerk Sauce

Cuban Black Bean Sauce

Banana Salsa

TOMATO-ORANGE SAUCE

Yield 3 cups *(6 half-cup servings)*

½ cup defatted chicken stock
1 cup low-sodium tomato juice
1 cup orange juice, freshly squeezed
2 teaspoons cornstarch dissolved in ¼ cup
chicken stock
Zest of 1 orange

ombine first 3 ingredients and bring to boil. Thicken with cornstarch and stock mixture. Add zest and stir for 1 minute.

Nutritional Data

PER SERVING:		EXCHANGES:	
Calories:	32	Milk:	0.0
Fat (gm):	0.2	Vegetable:	0.3
Sat. fat (gm):	trace	Fruit:	0.3
Cholesterol (mg):	0	Bread:	0.1
Sodium (mg):	69	Meat:	0.0
% Calories from fat:	6	Fat:	0.0

BAKED RED SNAPPER FILLETS
in Tomato-Orange Sauce

Serves 6
6 small red snapper fillets
3 cups *Tomato-Orange Sauce*
1 tablespoon fresh basil, chopped
2 oranges, thinly sliced

Place fillets in shallow baking pan. Pour ½ cup
Tomato-Orange Sauce over fillets. Evenly sprinkle
basil over fish. Top each fillet with 1 orange slice.
Bake in 350-degree oven 20-25 minutes. Serve with
remaining Tomato-Orange Sauce.

Nutritional Data
PER SERVING:

Calories:	271
Fat (gm):	3.2
Sat. fat (gm):	0.7
Cholesterol (mg):	80.7
Sodium (mg):	209
% Calories from fat:	11

EXCHANGES:

Milk:	0.0	Bread:	0.1
Veg.:	0.3	Meat:	7.6
Fruit:	0.7	Fat:	0.0

BEEF CUBES WITH NOODLES
in Tomato-Orange Sauce

Serves 6
1½ tablespoons canola oil
1½ lbs. extra-lean beef cubes (from round
    steak)
3 cups *Tomato-Orange Sauce*
1½ cups cooked spinach noodles

Heat oil in non-stick skillet until barely smoking.
Brown beef cubes on all sides and drain well. Pour
Tomato-Orange Sauce over beef cubes. Cover and
simmer 1 hour, adding water if sauce becomes too
thick. Serve with cooked spinach noodles.

Nutritional Data
PER SERVING:

Calories:	27
Fat (gm):	11.1
Sat. fat (gm):	2.4
Cholesterol (mg):	78.1
Sodium (mg):	144
% Calories from fat:	30

EXCHANGES:

Milk:	0.0	Bread:	0.6
Veg.:	0.3	Meat:	4
Fruit:	0.3	Fat:	0.7

ISLAND RUM-LIME SAUCE

Yield 3 cups (6 half-cup servings)

2 cups defatted chicken stock
¼ cup shallots, minced
2 large cloves garlic, minced
1 tablespoon cornstarch dissolved in ¼ cup water
2 tablespoons light rum
Juice of 1 lime
¼ cup parsley, minced
Salt and pepper to taste

Bring stock, shallots, and garlic to boil. Reduce heat and simmer 5 minutes. Thicken with cornstarch and water mixture. Add rum and boil 1 minute. Add lime juice and remove from heat. Season with parsley, salt, and pepper.

Nutritional Data

PER SERVING:		EXCHANGES:	
Calories:	39	Milk:	0.0
Fat (gm):	0.5	Vegetable:	0.3
Sat. fat (gm):	0.1	Fruit:	0.1
Cholesterol (mg):	0	Bread:	0.1
Sodium (mg):	261	Meat:	0.0
% Calories from fat:	11	Fat:	0.2

Fruited Island Pork Chops

Serves 12

3 tablespoons olive oil
6 large, boneless loin pork chops
¼ cup pimiento, chopped
¼ cup onion, minced
½ cup unsweetened pineapple chunks
½ cup unsweetened canned peach slices
½ cup fresh apple slices
½ cup fresh orange slices
¼ cup honey
3 cups *Island Rum-Lime Sauce*

Nutritional Data

PER SERVING:

Calories:	220
Fat (gm):	13.1
Sat. fat (gm):	4
Cholesterol (mg):	41.4
Sodium (mg):	162
% Calories from fat:	22

EXCHANGES:

Milk:	0.0	Bread:	0.1
Veg.:	0.4	Meat:	2.0
Fruit:	1.1	Fat:	1.5

Heat olive oil in non-stick skillet until barely smoking. Brown pork chops evenly on all sides. Combine remaining ingredients, and layer in bottom of large casserole.

Place browned chops atop fruit, vegetable, and honey mixture. Pour Island Rum-Lime Sauce over chops. Bake in 350-degree oven 20-30 minutes. Baste frequently with cooking juices. Cut pork chops in half lengthwise across the middle before serving.

Baked Barbados Red Snapper
in Island Rum-Lime Sauce

Serves 6

6 red snapper fillets
Aluminum foil
½ cup onion, thinly sliced into rings
½ cup green or red bell pepper, thinly sliced
1 tomato, peeled, seeded, chopped
1 teaspoon fresh basil, finely chopped
1 teaspoon fresh thyme, finely chopped
¼ teaspoon fresh oregano
3 cups *Island Rum-Lime Sauce*
2 limes, cut into 6 slices

Nutritional Data

PER SERVING:

Calories:	205
Fat (gm):	2.6
Sat. fat (gm):	0.6
Cholesterol (mg):	78.2
Sodium (mg):	396
% Calories from fat:	12

EXCHANGES:

Milk:	0.0	Bread:	0.1
Veg.:	0.7	Meat:	5.7
Fruit:	0.2	Fat:	0.2

Preheat oven to 350 degrees. Make 6 squares of aluminum foil, about 10 x 12 inches each. Place 1 fillet in center of each square. Evenly distribute vegetables across fish and sprinkle with herbs. Pour ½ cup of Island Rum-Lime Sauce over each fillet and top with lime slices.

To seal pouches, fold foil over fish and crimp edges. Bake at 350 degrees 25-30 minutes. Open carefully due to rising steam.

SPICY MANGO SAUCE

Yield 2 cups *(8 quarter-cup servings)*

2 ripe mangos
1 clove garlic
¼ cup onion, minced
1 teaspoon red pepper flakes
1 tablespoon chili powder
¼ cup honey
2 tablespoons wine vinegar

Peel mangos and cut flesh away from pit. Puree in food processor or blender with garlic. Add all remaining ingredients and bring mixture to boil. Reduce heat and simmer 1 minute. Can be served hot or cold.

Nutritional Data

PER SERVING:		EXCHANGES:	
Calories:	69	Milk:	0.0
Fat (gm):	0.2	Vegetable:	0.5
Sat. fat (gm):	trace	Fruit:	0.1
Cholesterol (mg):	0	Bread:	0.0
Sodium (mg):	1	Meat:	0.0
% Calories from fat:	1	Fat:	0.0

CHILLED SHRIMP AND MELON SKEWERS
with Spicy Mango Sauce

Serves 6

1½ cups cooked, chilled shrimp, peeled, deveined

1 cup melon balls (cantaloupe, honeydew, *or* watermelon)

2 cups *Spicy Mango Sauce*

6 wooden skewers, presoaked in cold water 20 minutes

Thread bamboo skewers with shrimp and melon balls. Brush on Spicy Mango Sauce, and serve remaining sauce as an accompaniment. Use a single shrimp and melon ball for an appetizer-size serving.

Nutritional Data

PER SERVING:

Calories:	161
Fat (gm):	1.3
Sat. fat (gm):	0.3
Cholesterol (mg):	86.3
Sodium (mg):	95
% Calories from fat:	7

EXCHANGES:

Milk:	0.0	Bread:	0.0
Veg.:	0.1	Meat:	1.7
Fruit:	1.5	Fat:	0.0

TROPICAL CHICKEN "WINGS"

Serves 10

3 lbs. chicken thighs, skin removed

12 ozs. canned crushed pineapple

2 cups *Spicy Mango Sauce*

Sear chicken thighs on hot grill 2-3 minutes but do not cook through. Pour pineapple over chicken. Top with 2 cups Spicy Mango Sauce. Bake in 400-degree oven 35-40 minutes, basting often.

Nutritional Data

PER SERVING:

Calories:	236
Fat (gm):	5.5
Sat. fat (gm):	1.4
Cholesterol (mg):	113
Sodium (mg):	119
% Calories from fat:	21

EXCHANGES:

Milk:	0.0	Bread:	0.0
Veg.:	0.0	Meat:	3.9
Fruit:	1.1	Fat:	0.0

Papaya Ginger Sauce

Yield 2 cups (8 quarter-cup servings)

1 ripe papaya
1 clove garlic, minced
¼ cup onion, minced
1 tablespoon fresh ginger, grated
1 cup papaya juice (apricot or passion fruit juice
   may be substituted)
2 tablespoons red wine vinegar
2 tablespoons low-sodium soy sauce
   Salt and pepper to taste
2 tablespoons chives, minced

P uree papaya, garlic, onion, and ginger in food processor or blender. Add fruit juice, vinegar, soy sauce, salt, and pepper. Bring to boil and simmer 2-3 minutes. Add chives.

Nutritional Data

PER SERVING:		EXCHANGES:	
Calories:	57	Milk:	0.0
Fat (gm):	0.2	Vegetable:	0.3
Sat. fat (gm):	trace	Fruit:	0.7
Cholesterol (mg):	0	Bread:	0.0
Sodium (mg):	409	Meat:	0.0
% Calories from fat:	1	Fat:	0.0

STIR-FRIED SEA SCALLOPS
in Papaya Ginger Sauce

Serves 6

  2 tablespoons canola oil
1½ lbs. sea or bay scallops
  ½ lb. snow peas
  1 lb. red bell pepper, cut into thin strips
  1 4-oz. can water chestnuts
  2 cups *Papaya Ginger Sauce*

Heat oil in wok or non-stick skillet until barely smoking. Separately stir-fry scallops, snow peas, pepper, and water chestnuts in successive batches. Be sure to cook until vegetables are just crisp and scallops slightly underdone.

When vegetables and scallops are ready, combine in wok, add sauce, and bring to boil. Serve with or without hot rice.

Nutritional Data

PER SERVING:

Calories:	220
Fat (gm):	5.7
Sat. fat (gm):	0.5
Cholesterol (mg):	37.4
Sodium (mg):	460
% Calories from fat:	23

EXCHANGES:

Milk:	0.0	Bread:	0.0
Veg.:	2.1	Meat:	4.0
Fruit:	0.5	Fat:	0.9

JAMAICAN JERK SAUCE

Yield 2 cups *(8 quarter-cup servings)*

1 large onion
1 complete garlic bulb, peeled and blanched in boiling water
¼ cup pimiento
¼ cup pickled jalapeño
¼ cup honey
1 tablespoon Worcestershire sauce
1 teaspoon fresh thyme
1 teaspoon cinnamon
½ teaspoon nutmeg
½ teaspoon black pepper
¼ teaspoon cayenne pepper
1 teaspoon chili or Tabasco sauce
2 tablespoons olive oil

uree all ingredients in food processor or blender.

Nutritional Data

PER SERVING:		EXCHANGES:	
Calories:	79	Milk:	0.0
Fat (gm):	3.5	Vegetable:	0.6
Sat. fat (gm):	0.5	Fruit:	1.1
Cholesterol (mg):	0	Bread:	0.0
Sodium (mg):	99	Meat:	0.0
% Calories from fat:	15	Fat:	1.3

JAMAICAN CHICKEN "WINGS"

Serves 10

4 lbs. chicken thighs, skin removed
1 cup *Jamaican Jerk Sauce* thinned with
  1 cup water to make 2 cups

Marinate "wings" in Jamaican Jerk Sauce at least 1
hour. Place in roasting pan, one layer of wings at a
time. Pour sauce over chicken, and roast in hot
oven at 400 degrees 35-40 minutes.

Nutritional Data

PER SERVING:

Calories:	222
Fat (gm):	9.2
Sat. fat (gm):	2
Cholesterol (mg):	99.3
Sodium (mg):	210
% Calories from fat:	30

EXCHANGES:

Milk:	0.0	Bread:	0.0
Veg.:	0.2	Meat:	5.3
Fruit:	0.4	Fat:	0.3

KINGSTON GRILLED CHICKEN TENDERLOINS
with Jamaican Jerk Sauce

Serves 6

3 lbs. chicken tenderloins, skinless
2 medium size red onions, quartered
2 large green bell peppers, sliced into 6 rings
2 large ears of corn, cut in half
2 cups *Jamaican Jerk Sauce*

Place chicken and vegetables in shallow pan, and
cover with Jamaican Jerk Sauce. Marinate at least 1
hour. Grill over low to moderate fire 30-45 minutes,
turning occasionally and basting until chicken is
cooked through.

Nutritional Data

PER SERVING:

Calories:	287
Fat (gm):	5.9
Sat. fat (gm):	1.1
Cholesterol (mg):	98.6
Sodium (mg):	121
% Calories from fat:	19

EXCHANGES:

Milk:	0.0	Bread:	0.2
Veg.:	0.8	Meat:	4.3
Fruit:	0.5	Fat:	0.7

CUBAN BLACK BEAN SAUCE

Yield 3 cups (6 half-cup servings)

2 cups cooked black beans
1 jalapeño pepper, seeded
1 cup defatted chicken stock
1 large clove garlic, minced
¼ cup dry sherry

Puree all ingredients except sherry in food processor or blender. Bring to boil and reduce heat, simmering 5 minutes. Stir often, adding water if sauce becomes too thick. Stir in sherry and return to boil for 1 minute to evaporate alcohol.

Nutritional Data

PER SERVING:		EXCHANGES:	
Calories:	90	Milk:	0.0
Fat (gm):	0.6	Vegetable:	0.0
Sat. fat (gm):	0.1	Fruit:	0.0
Cholesterol (mg):	0	Bread:	0.9
Sodium (mg):	151	Meat:	0.1
% Calories from fat:	5	Fat:	0.1

CHICKEN AND BLACK BEAN QUESADILLAS

Serves 6

3 tablespoons olive oil

1½ lbs. boneless chicken breasts, skin removed, cut into strips

1 green bell pepper, cut into 1-inch strips

1 medium onion, thinly sliced

1 clove garlic, minced

Juice of 1 lime

3 cups *Cuban Black Bean Sauce*, divided

6 flour tortillas

1 cup low-fat sharp Cheddar cheese, shredded

Nutritional Data

PER SERVING:

Calories:	375
Fat (gm):	11.3
Sat. fat (gm):	2.5
Cholesterol (mg):	69.7
Sodium (mg):	467
% Calories from fat:	23

EXCHANGES:

Milk:	0.0	Bread:	2.4
Veg.:	0.4	Meat:	3.6
Fruit:	0.1	Fat:	1.5

Heat olive oil in non-stick skillet until barely smoking. Sauté chicken strips until lightly browned. Add green pepper slices, onion, garlic, and lime juice. Cook 2-3 minutes. Add 1 cup Cuban Black Bean sauce, and simmer 2 minutes.

Spoon ¼ cup of mixture onto center of each tortilla and roll up. Place in casserole that can accommodate all 6 tortillas in one layer. Pour remaining 2 cups Cuban Black Bean Sauce around tortillas and across center. Sprinkle with cheese, and cook in 350-degree oven 15-20 minutes.

GRILLED TURKEY CUTLETS
with Cuban Black Bean Sauce

Serves 6

1½ lbs. turkey cutlets, *or* turkey medallions

¼ cup non-fat Italian dressing, vinaigrette style

1 clove garlic, minced

Juice of 1 lime

2 cups *Cuban Black Bean Sauce*

Nutritional Data

PER SERVING:

Calories:	352
Fat (gm):	4.9
Sat. fat (gm):	1.6
Cholesterol (mg):	96
Sodium (mg):	478
% Calories from fat:	14

EXCHANGES:

Milk:	0.0	Bread:	1.8
Veg.:	0.0	Meat:	3.0
Fruit:	0.1	Fat:	0.8

Spread Italian dressing, garlic, and lime juice evenly over turkey and marinate at least 1 hour. Grill very quickly over medium-hot coals. Do not overcook or meat will become dry. Serve with Cuban Black Bean Sauce as an accompaniment.

BANANA SALSA

Yield 3 cups *(6 half-cup servings)*

2 large, firm bananas, finely minced and tossed in ¼ cup fresh lime juice
¼ cup pimiento
¼ cup jalapeño pepper, seeded, minced
¼ cup red onion, minced
¼ cup honey
¼ cup green onions with tops, finely minced
¼ fresh lime juice

 Combine all ingredients and refrigerate at least 1 hour.

Nutritional Data

PER SERVING:		EXCHANGES:	
Calories:	87	Milk:	0.0
Fat (gm):	0.3	Vegetable:	0.3
Sat. fat (gm):	0.1	Fruit:	1.3
Cholesterol (mg):	0	Bread:	0.0
Sodium (mg):	86	Meat:	0.0
% Calories from fat:	3	Fat:	0.0

APPLE, PEAR, AND PAPAYA QUESADILLAS
with Banana Salsa

Serves 6

4 flour tortillas
1 cup fresh apple slices
1 cup fresh pear slices
1 cup fresh papaya slices
1 cup low-fat mozzarella cheese, shredded
2 cups *Banana Salsa*

Preheat oven to 350 degrees. Evenly distribute fruit and cheese across tortillas. Bake in 350-degree oven 6-10 minutes. Fold each tortilla in half and cut into thirds. Serve with Banana Salsa as dipping sauce.

Nutritional Data

PER SERVING:

Calories:	264
Fat (gm):	6.1
Sat. fat (gm):	3.1
Cholesterol (mg):	10.2
Sodium (mg):	353
% Calories from fat:	18

EXCHANGES:

Milk:	0.0	Bread:	0.9
Veg.:	0.9	Meat:	0.8
Fruit:	2.3	Fat:	0.4

GRILLED RED SNAPPER
with Banana Salsa

Serves 6

6 red snapper fillets
   Juice of 1 lemon
4 tablespoons olive oil
3 cups *Banana Salsa*

Pour juice over fish and let marinate 30 minutes. Brush fish with olive oil, and grill over medium-hot coals 3-4 minutes on each side. Spoon Banana Salsa across top of fish and serve.

Nutritional Data

PER SERVING:

Calories:	334
Fat (gm):	14.8
Sat. fat (gm):	2.8
Cholesterol (mg):	53
Sodium (mg):	208
% Calories from fat:	30

EXCHANGES:

Milk:	0.0	Bread:	0.0
Veg.:	0.3	Meat:	4.8
Fruit:	1.4	Fat:	1.7

8.
MEXICAN AND LATIN AMERICAN SAUCES AND MARINADES

Veggie Salsa

♦

Shrimp and Chili Sauce

♦

Pineapple Picante

♦

Peppers, Corn, and Scallion Salsa

♦

Melon Tequila Salsa

♦

Light Jalapeño Mayonnaise

♦

Portuguese Garlic Sauce

VEGGIE SALSA

Yield 3 cups *(12 quarter-cup servings)*

1 zucchini, diced
1 yellow squash, diced
1 large red onion, diced
1 red bell pepper, diced
1 green bell pepper, diced
1 large carrot, diced
3 large tomatoes, chopped
3 tablespoons red wine vinegar
1 bunch green onions, thinly sliced
1 cup low-sodium tomato juice
3 tablespoons olive oil
  Salt and pepper to taste

ix ingredients and let stand at least 1 hour.

Nutritional Data

PER SERVING:		EXCHANGES:	
Calories:	56.5	Milk:	0.0
Fat (gm):	3.6	Vegetable:	0.9
Sat. fat (gm):	0.5	Fruit:	0.0
Cholesterol (mg):	0	Bread:	0.0
Sodium (mg):	7.9	Meat:	0.0
% Calories from fat:	10	Fat:	0.7

BLACK BEAN AND CHICKEN BURRITOS

Serves 6

2 cups cooked black beans, drained
2 cups cooked chicken meat, shredded
3 cups *Veggie Salsa*, divided
6 flour tortillas
1 cup low-fat Monterey Jack cheese

Preheat oven to 350 degrees. Combine beans, chicken, and 1 cup Veggie Salsa and thoroughly mix. Fill each tortilla with ½ cup bean mixture and roll up. Place in casserole.

    Spoon 1 cup Veggie Salsa around and across the burritos. Evenly distribute the low-fat Monterey Jack across top, and bake at 350 degrees 20-30 minutes until cheese is melted. Serve remaining cup of Veggie Salsa on the side.

Nutritional Data

PER SERVING:

Calories:	392
Fat (gm):	14.1
Sat. fat (gm):	3.7
Cholesterol (mg):	54
Sodium (mg):	333
% Calories from fat:	29

EXCHANGES:

Milk:	0.0	Bread:	2.2
Veg.:	1.8	Meat:	2.8
Fruit:	0.0	Fat:	1.8

CHICKEN AND SPINACH QUESADILLAS
with Veggie Salsa

Serves 6

4 flour tortillas
1 cup low-fat mozzarella cheese, shredded
1 cup spinach leaves
1 cup boneless cooked chicken, skin removed, finely chopped
3 cups *Veggie Salsa*

Preheat oven to 350 degrees. Distribute cheese evenly on each tortilla. Cover cheese with spinach leaves. Cover spinach with chicken. Place quesadillas on cookie sheet and bake 6 minutes or until cheese is melting and tortilla edges are brown. Fold each tortilla in half, and then cut into thirds. Serve with Veggie Salsa.

Nutritional Data

PER SERVING:

Calories:	275
Fat (gm):	12.5
Sat. fat (gm):	3.4
Cholesterol (mg):	32.1
Sodium (mg):	259
% Calories from fat:	30

EXCHANGES:

Milk:	0.0	Bread:	0.9
Veg.:	1.8	Meat:	1.7
Fruit:	0.0	Fat:	1.7

SHRIMP AND CHILI SAUCE

Yield 3 cups (12 quarter-cup servings)

1 small can mild green chilies
2 cups canned tomatoes, chopped
1 bunch fresh parsley, minced
1 large clove garlic, minced
¼ cup onion, minced
2 tablespoons fresh basil
1 teaspoon fresh oregano
2 tablespoons red wine vinegar
1 tablespoon olive oil
   Salt and pepper to taste
1½ cups cooked fresh shrimp, diced

ix all ingredients and let stand 1 hour before serving.

Nutritional Data

PER SERVING:		EXCHANGES:	
Calories:	94.6	Milk:	0.0
Fat (gm):	2.6	Vegetable:	0.4
Sat. fat (gm):	0.3	Fruit:	0.0
Cholesterol (mg):	24	Bread:	0.0
Sodium (mg):	100	Meat:	1.2
% Calories from fat:	12	Fat:	0.4

CRAB AND HAVARTI DILL QUESADILLAS

Serves 8

1 cup fresh crab meat, cooked and picked through for shell
1 cup pimiento
4 flour tortillas
1½ cups low-fat havarti dill cheese, grated, *or* other low-fat cheese
2 cups *Shrimp and Chili Sauce*

Preheat oven to 350 degrees. Combine crab and pimiento and distribute over tortillas. Spread cheese evenly on all 4 tortillas. Place quesadillas on cookie sheet and bake 6 minutes or until cheese is melting and tortilla edges are brown. Fold tortillas in half, and cut each into thirds. Serve with Shrimp and Chili Sauce.

Nutritional Data

PER SERVING:

Calories:	252
Fat (gm):	12.6
Sat. fat (gm):	4.1
Cholesterol (mg):	89
Sodium (mg):	393
% Calories from fat:	22

EXCHANGES:

Milk:	0.0	Bread:	0.7
Veg.:	0.8	Meat:	2.5
Fruit:	0.0	Fat:	1.6

TROUT SANTA FE
with Shrimp and Chili Sauce

Serves 6

5 tablespoons Santa Fe Seasoning (see recipe below)
6 whole trouts (about 1¼ lbs. each), butter-flied and deboned
4 tablespoons olive oil
2½ cups *Shrimp and Chili Sauce*

Santa Fe Seasoning

1 tablespoon garlic powder
1 tablespoon onion powder
1 tablespoon white pepper
1 tablespoon paprika
1 tablespoon chili powder

Nutritional Data

PER SERVING:

Calories:	289
Fat (gm):	20.8
Sat. fat (gm):	3.7
Cholesterol (mg):	97
Sodium (mg):	244
% Calories from fat:	30

EXCHANGES:

Milk:	0.0	Bread:	0.0
Veg.:	0.8	Meat:	5.6
Fruit:	0.0	Fat:	3.5

Combine all ingredients for Santa Fe Seasoning and mix well. Sprinkle each trout with equal amounts of seasoning. Brush both sides of fish with olive oil.

Place trout, skin side up, on fish grill or under broiler. Cover with foil and cook 2½ minutes per side. Spoon Shrimp and Chili Sauce across each trout and serve.

PINEAPPLE PICANTE

Yield 3 cups *(6 half-cup servings)*

2 cups pineapple chunks
¼ cup onion, minced
1 clove garlic, minced
1 jalapeño pepper, diced
2 tablespoons honey
    Juice and zest of 1 lime
1 bunch green onions, finely sliced
    Salt and pepper to taste

ombine all ingredients and let stand for at least 1 hour before serving.

Nutritional Data

PER SERVING:		EXCHANGES:	
Calories:	56	Milk:	0.0
Fat (gm):	0.3	Vegetable:	0.2
Sat. fat (gm):	trace	Fruit:	0.7
Cholesterol (mg):	0	Bread:	0.0
Sodium (mg):	23	Meat:	0.0
% Calories from fat:	4	Fat:	0.0

GRILLED SWORDFISH SKEWERS
with Pineapple Picante

Serves 6 *(2 skewers each)*

1½ lbs. swordfish, cut into 1-inch cubes
1 cup fresh pineapple, cut into 1-inch cubes
1 cup red or green bell pepper, cut into 1-inch squares
1 cup red onion, cut into 1-inch squares
12 wooden skewers, presoaked in cold water 20 minutes
3 cups Pineapple Marinade (see recipe below)
1 cup *Pineapple Picante*

Pineapple Marinade

2 cups pineapple juice
1 cup white wine
1 jalapeño pepper
1 tablespoon fresh basil
2 tablespoons olive oil

Nutritional Data

PER SERVING:

Calories:	339
Fat (gm):	9.7
Sat. fat (gm):	1.9
Cholesterol (mg):	44.2
Sodium (mg):	136
% Calories from fat:	25

EXCHANGES:

Milk:	0.0	Bread:	0.0
Veg.:	1.1	Meat:	4.0
Fruit:	1.6	Fat:	1.5

Thread swordfish, fruit, and vegetables onto wooden skewers, alternating the different colors. Combine Marinade ingredients, and marinate assembled skewers 1 hour. Grill over medium-hot coals until done, 3-4 minutes on each side. Serve on cooked rice (not included in nutritional data) with Pineapple Picante as accompaniment.

MEXICAN BEER SHRIMP
with Pineapple Picante

Serves 6

1 12-oz. can light beer
2 cloves garlic, crushed
1 tablespoon chili powder
1 tablespoon cayenne pepper
1 lime, thinly sliced
1 lb. shrimp, peeled and deveined
3 cups *Pineapple Picante*

Nutritional Data

PER SERVING:

Calories:	179
Fat (gm):	2.2
Sat. fat (gm):	0.4
Cholesterol (mg):	99.6
Sodium (mg):	183
% Calories from fat:	10

EXCHANGES:

Milk:	0.0	Bread:	0.0
Veg.:	0.2	Meat:	2.9
Fruit:	0.8	Fat:	0.3

Bring first 5 ingredients to boil. Reduce heat and simmer 15 minutes. Add shrimp, return to boil, and cook 3-4 minutes until done. Chill in liquid, and serve with Pineapple Picante as dipping sauce.

PEPPERS, CORN, AND SCALLION SALSA

Yield 3 cups (6 half-cup servings)

1 red bell pepper, diced
1 yellow bell pepper, diced
1 green bell pepper, diced
1 cup cooked corn kernels
1 bunch green onions, finely minced
1 large clove garlic, minced
2 tablespoons red wine vinegar
1 tablespoon brown sugar
   Sugar Twin Brown Sugar substitute equivalent
   to 1 tablespoon brown sugar
1 tablespoon fresh basil
2 tablespoons olive oil
   Salt and pepper to taste

ix all ingredients and let stand at least 1 hour before serving.

Nutritional Data

PER SERVING:		EXCHANGES:	
Calories:	92	Milk:	0.0
Fat (gm):	4.9	Vegetable:	0.5
Sat. fat (gm):	0.7	Fruit:	0.2
Cholesterol (mg):	0	Bread:	0.3
Sodium (mg):	7	Meat:	0.0
% Calories from fat:	23	Fat:	0.9

SAUTÉED SALMON
with Peppers, Corn, and Scallion Salsa

Serves 12

- 6 thick salmon fillets
- ½ cup cornmeal
- ½ teaspoon cayenne pepper
  Non-stick cooking spray
- 1 tablespoon olive oil
- 2 cups *Peppers, Corn, and Scallion Salsa*

Combine cornmeal and cayenne. Coat salmon fillets evenly with mixture. Spray skillet with non-stick spray. Heat olive oil in skillet until barely smoking. Sauté salmon in oil 4-5 minutes per side. Slice each fillet in half lengthwise. Spoon Peppers, Corn, and Scallion Salsa on top.

Nutritional Data

PER SERVING:

Calories:	343
Fat (gm):	15.5
Sat. fat (gm):	2.6
Cholesterol (mg):	100
Sodium (mg):	92
% Calories from fat:	30

EXCHANGES:

Milk:	0.0	Bread:	0.4
Veg.:	0.3	Meat:	6.9
Fruit:	0.1	Fat:	0.9

GRILLED CATFISH FILLETS
with Peppers, Corn, and Scallion Salsa

Serves 6

- 1½ lbs. catfish fillets
- 1¼ cups Catfish Marinade (see recipe below)
- 3 cups *Peppers, Corn, and Scallion Salsa*

Catfish Marinade

- 1 cup white wine
- ¼ cup low-sodium soy sauce
- 1 clove garlic, crushed
- 1 tablespoon paprika
- ¼ teaspoon cayenne
- ¾ tablespoon olive oil

Nutritional Data

PER SERVING:

Calories:	228
Fat (gm):	9
Sat. fat (gm):	1.7
Cholesterol (mg):	54.8
Sodium (mg):	589
% Calories from fat:	30

EXCHANGES:

Milk:	0.0	Bread:	0.3
Veg.:	0.5	Meat:	1.7
Fruit:	0.2	Fat:	1.8

Combine ingredients for Catfish Marinade, and marinate catfish fillets 1 hour. Grill over hot coals on fish grill, 4 minutes per side. Spoon salsa across fillets and serve.

MELON TEQUILA SALSA

Yield 3 cups *(12 quarter-cup servings)*

2 cups mixed melon, finely diced (cantaloupe, honeydew, watermelon, etc.)
1 large clove garlic, minced
¼ cup onion, minced
1 teaspoon hot pepper flakes
2 tablespoons honey
   Juice of 1 lime
2 tablespoons tequila
¼ cup olive oil
   Salt and pepper to taste

ix ingredients well and refrigerate 1 hour before serving.

Nutritional Data

PER SERVING:		EXCHANGES:	
Calories:	69	Milk:	0.0
Fat (gm):	4.1	Vegetable:	0.5
Sat. fat (gm):	0.6	Fruit:	0.4
Cholesterol (mg):	0	Bread:	0.0
Sodium (mg):	9	Meat:	0.0
% Calories from fat:	14	Fat:	1.0

CHARCOAL GRILLED SHRIMP
with Melon Tequila Salsa

Serves 12

- 2 lbs. fresh medium shrimp
- 12 wooden skewers, presoaked in cold water 20 minutes
- 2 green bell peppers, cut into 1-inch cubes
- 2 red onions, cut into 1-inch cubes
- 3 tablespoons canola oil
  Juice of 1 lime
  Salt and pepper to taste
- 3 cups *Melon Tequila Salsa*

Nutritional Data

PER SERVING:

Calories:	198
Fat (gm):	9.6
Sat. fat (gm):	1.7
Cholesterol (mg):	100
Sodium (mg):	135
% Calories from fat:	13

EXCHANGES:

Milk:	0.0	Bread:	0.0
Veg.:	2.4	Meat:	3.1
Fruit:	0.2	Fat:	1.7

Peel and devein shrimp. Thread one-twelfth of shrimp onto each skewer, interspersing with pepper and onion cubes. Brush with canola oil. Grill over hot charcoal about 2 minutes per side. Remove shrimp from grill and sprinkle with lime juice, salt, and pepper. Serve hot with chilled Melon Tequila Salsa.

MELON AND CHICKEN SALAD

Serves 4

- 2 ripe cantaloupes, *or* honeydews
- ¾ cup non-fat mayonnaise
- 2¾ cups *Melon Tequila Salsa*, divided
- 2 cups boneless cooked chicken, skin removed
- ¼ cup celery, diced
- ¼ cup red onion, diced

Nutritional Data

PER SERVING:

Calories:	387
Fat (gm):	15
Sat. fat (gm):	2.2
Cholesterol (mg):	65.7
Sodium (mg):	618
% Calories from fat:	30

EXCHANGES:

Milk:	0.0	Bread:	0.0
Veg.:	0.3	Meat:	2.9
Fruit:	2.1	Fat:	3.0

Cut melons in half, remove seeds, and scoop out melon balls. Combine non-fat mayonnaise and 2 cups Melon Tequila Salsa. Toss chicken, melon balls, celery, and onion with mayo and salsa mixture. Chill and present in hollowed-out melon halves, with remainder of salsa in separate serving dish.

LIGHT JALAPEÑO MAYONNAISE

Yield 3 cups *(12 quarter-cup servings)*

2½ cups non-fat mayonnaise
2 tablespoons chili powder
2 tablespoons honey
2 tablespoons lime juice
1 jalapeño, seeded, finely minced

Combine all ingredients and refrigerate at least 1 hour before serving.

Nutritional Data

PER SERVING:		EXCHANGES:	
Calories:	47	Milk:	0.0
Fat (gm):	trace	Vegetable:	0.0
Sat. fat (gm):	trace	Fruit:	0.8
Cholesterol (mg):	0	Bread:	0.0
Sodium (mg):	574	Meat:	0.0
% Calories from fat:	1	Fat:	0.0

CRAB CAKES OLÉ
with Light Jalapeño Mayonnaise

Serves 6

2 cups fresh crab meat, cooked and picked over for shells

¼ cup onion, minced

¼ cup low-sodium dill pickle, minced

1 cup breadcrumbs from reduced-calorie stale bread, divided

1 tablespoon Old Bay, *or* other crab seasoning

¼ cup non-fat low-sodium mayonnaise

2 egg whites

3 cups *Light Jalapeño Mayonnaise*

Nutritional Data
PER SERVING:

Calories:	202
Fat (gm):	1.5
Sat. fat (gm):	0.3
Cholesterol (mg):	36.3
Sodium (mg):	799
% Calories from fat:	6

EXCHANGES:

Milk:	0.0	Bread:	0.8
Veg.:	0.2	Meat:	1.0
Fruit:	1.7	Fat:	0.0

Mix together all ingredients, except Light Jalapeño Mayonnaise, reserving ½ cup breadcrumbs. Form mixture into 6 crab cakes. Coat cakes with remaining breadcrumbs.

Apply non-stick spray to non-stick skillet and heat. Brown crab cakes in skillet, and serve with Light Jalapeño Mayonnaise.

BEEF PINWHEELS
with Light Jalapeño Mayonnaise

Serves 6

½ large ripe avocado, peeled, pitted, and cut into 6 slices

Juice of 1 lemon

6 thin slices lean roast beef (1 lb.)

2 cups *Light Jalapeño Mayonnaise*

6 lettuce leaves

6 low-sodium dill pickle spears

Toothpicks

Nutritional Data
PER SERVING:

Calories:	297
Fat (gm):	14
Sat. fat (gm):	4.1
Cholesterol (mg):	50
Sodium (mg):	799
% Calories from fat:	30

EXCHANGES:

Milk:	0.0	Bread:	0.0
Veg.:	0.5	Meat:	2.7
Fruit:	1.8	Fat:	1.0

Toss avocado slices in lemon juice to prevent discoloring. Thinly spread slices of roast beef with Light Jalapeño Mayonnaise, and top with lettuce leaf. Top lettuce with 1 dill pickle spear and avocado slice. Roll up beef jellyroll style and secure with toothpick. For appetizers, cut rolls into bite-size mini-rolls.

PORTUGUESE GARLIC SAUCE

Yield 3 cups *(6 half-cup servings)*

2 large whole garlic bulbs, cloves peeled and
   separated
2 cups defatted chicken stock
1 tablespoon cornstarch dissolved in ¼ cup
   sherry

Bring 1 quart water to boil and blanch garlic 5 minutes. Drain
and reserve. Bring stock to boil and add blanched garlic. Reduce
heat and simmer 1 hour, adding more stock or water if liquid evaporates.
Add cornstarch and sherry mixture, and cook until thickened, stirring constantly.

Nutritional Data

PER SERVING:		EXCHANGES:	
Calories:	31	Milk:	0.0
Fat (gm):	484	Vegetable:	0.0
Sat. fat (gm):	0.1	Fruit:	0.0
Cholesterol (mg):	0	Bread:	0.1
Sodium (mg):	260	Meat:	0.0
% Calories from fat:	14	Fat:	0.1

FLAMENCO CHICKEN
with Portuguese Garlic Sauce

Serves 6

6 chicken breasts, skinless and boneless
1 cup Flamenco Marinade (see recipe below)
3 cups *Portuguese Garlic Sauce*

Flamenco Marinade

1 onion
2 large cloves garlic
  Juice of 1 lemon
¼ tablespoon saffron
  Salt and pepper to taste

Nutritional Data			
PER SERVING:			
Calories:	170		
Fat (gm):	2		
Sat. fat (gm):	0.5		
Cholesterol (mg):	68.4		
Sodium (mg):	338		
% Calories from fat:	11		
EXCHANGES:			
Milk:	0.0	Bread:	0.1
Veg.:	0.3	Meat:	3.0
Fruit:	0.1	Fat:	0.1

Preheat oven to 350 degrees. Puree ingredients for Flamenco Marinade in food processor or blender. Coat chicken well with puree. Marinate at least 1 hour.

Bake chicken at 350 degrees 1 hour. Turn oven up to 425 degrees and bake another 10-15 minutes until juices run clear. Serve with Portuguese Garlic Sauce.

VEAL CHOPS AU FROMAGE
with Blue Cheese and Portuguese Garlic Sauce

Serves 12

6 large, extra-lean veal chops
5 tablespoons canola oil
6 teaspoons blue cheese
3 cups *Portuguese Garlic Sauce*

Nutritional Data			
PER SERVING:			
Calories:	187		
Fat (gm):	12		
Sat. fat (gm):	3.5		
Cholesterol (mg):	48.3		
Sodium (mg):	182		
% Calories from fat:	30		
EXCHANGES:			
Milk:	0.0	Bread:	0.0
Veg.:	0.0	Meat:	1.7
Fruit:	0.0	Fat:	1.2

Generously brush oil on grill surface and chops so meat won't stick during cooking. Grill chops over medium heat 8-10 minutes on each side. Toward end of grilling, place 1 teaspoon blue cheese on top of each chop.

Cover grill until cheese is warmed and slightly melting. Cut each chop lengthwise across the middle before serving. Serve with Portuguese Garlic Sauce spooned generously on each chop.

9.
ALL-AMERICAN SAUCES AND MARINADES

◆
Cherry Wine Sauce
◆
Rice, Onion, and Mushroom Sauce
◆
Thick and Hearty Mushroom Sauce
◆
Light Tartar Sauce
◆
Savory Raisin Sauce
◆
Lemon Artichoke Sauce
◆
Apple-Shallot Sauce

CHERRY WINE SAUCE

Yield 3 cups (12 quarter-cup servings)

3/4 cup powdered sugar
1/4 cup red wine vinegar
 1 cup rose wine
 1 cup defatted chicken stock
 1 cup fresh, *or* canned, cherries, pitted and
   roughly chopped

In heavy sauce pan, cook powdered sugar over high heat until melted and slightly browned. Add vinegar, wine, and stock and bring to boil. Reduce sauce over heat until slightly thickened, 8-10 minutes. Add cherries and heat thoroughly.

Nutritional Data

PER SERVING:		EXCHANGES:	
Calories:	56	Milk:	0.0
Fat (gm):	0.3	Vegetable:	0.0
Sat. fat (gm):	0.1	Fruit:	0.6
Cholesterol (mg):	0	Bread:	0.0
Sodium (mg):	66	Meat:	0.0
% Calories from fat:	3	Fat:	0.3

ROASTED TURKEY BREAST
with Cherry Wine Sauce

Serves 6

1½ lb. pkg. turkey breast meat
2 cloves garlic, minced
2 cups rose wine
3 cups *Cherry Wine Sauce*

Preheat oven to 350 degrees. Remove turkey skin and rub meat with garlic. Pour wine over turkey, and roast according to package instructions. Baste often to prevent drying. Serve with Cherry Wine Sauce.

Nutritional Data

PER SERVING:

Calories:	300
Fat (gm):	2.9
Sat. fat (gm):	1.8
Cholesterol (mg):	75
Sodium (mg):	210
% Calories from fat:	20

EXCHANGES:

Milk:	0.0	Bread:	0.0
Veg.:	0.0	Meat:	2.6
Fruit:	1.2	Fat:	2.0

GAME HENS STUFFED WITH CORN BREAD
and Cherry Wine Sauce

Serves 6

6 small game hens, skin removed
  Stuffing (see recipe below)
1 clove garlic
2 cups rose wine
3 cups *Cherry Wine Sauce*

Stuffing

1 clove garlic
4 cups stale corn bread, crumbled
¼ cup onion
1 clove garlic, minced
¼ cup celery, diced
¼ cup carrot, diced
½ cup mushrooms, sliced
1 tablespoon sage
1 tablespoon thyme
¼ cup defatted chicken stock
1 egg white

Nutritional Data

PER SERVING:

Calories:	33
Fat (gm):	2.4
Sat. fat (gm):	0.6
Cholesterol (mg):	43.8
Sodium (mg):	475
% Calories from fat:	7

EXCHANGES:

Milk:	0.0	Bread:	0.9
Veg.:	0.1	Meat:	2.0
Fruit:	1.2	Fat:	2.0

Preheat oven to 350 degrees. Combine Stuffing ingredients and divide evenly, stuffing birds loosely. Rub hens with garlic. Pour wine over hens, and cook in 350-degree oven 45 minutes to 1 hour. Baste often. Serve with Cherry Wine Sauce.

Rice, Onion, and Mushroom Sauce

Yield 3 cups *(6 half-cup servings)*

1 cup cooked rice
1 cup onion, diced
1 cup mushrooms, sliced
1½ cups defatted chicken stock
½ cup white wine
Salt and pepper to taste
1 tablespoon dried thyme

Combine rice, onion, and mushrooms. Partially puree mixture in food processor or blender. Add stock and wine. Pour into saucepan and bring to boil. Add salt, pepper, and thyme.

Nutritional Data

PER SERVING:		EXCHANGES:	
Calories:	81	Milk:	0.0
Fat (gm):	0.5	Vegetable:	0.4
Sat. fat (gm):	0.1	Fruit:	0.0
Cholesterol (mg):	0	Bread:	0.6
Sodium (mg):	196	Meat:	0.0
% Calories from fat:	6	Fat:	0.3

DOWN HOME PORK CHOPS
with Rice, Onion, and Mushroom Sauce

Serves 6

2 cups cooked white rice
1 cup onion, diced
1 cup mushrooms, sliced
Non-stick cooking spray
2 tablespoons canola oil
6 extra-lean pork loin chops
Salt and pepper to taste
3 cups *Rice, Onion, and Mushroom Sauce,* divided

Nutritional Data

PER SERVING:

Calories:	354
Fat (gm):	13.1
Sat. fat (gm):	2.1
Cholesterol (mg):	55.6
Sodium (mg):	243
% Calories from fat:	30

EXCHANGES:

Milk:	0.0	Bread:	1.7
Veg.:	0.9	Meat:	2.4
Fruit:	0.0	Fat:	1.3

Preheat oven to 325 degrees. Combine rice, onion, and mushrooms, and spread in shallow baking dish. Spray non-stick skillet, and lightly coat with oil. Brown chops on all sides. Season with salt and pepper if desired.

Place browned chops on top of rice mixture. Pour 2 cups Rice, Onion, and Mushroom Sauce over chops and spread evenly. Cover with foil, and bake in 325-degree oven 30-45 minutes until done. Serve remaining sauce on the side.

BAKED CUBE STEAKS
with Rice, Onion, and Mushroom Sauce

Serves 6

3 tablespoons canola oil
6 cube steaks
2 cups *Rice, Onion, and Mushroom Sauce*

Preheat oven to 325 degrees. Brush non-stick skillet with oil, and brown steaks on both sides. Place in shallow baking dish, and cover evenly with Rice, Onion, and Mushroom Sauce.

Cover with foil and bake until steaks are tender, 45 minutes to 1 hour. Add water to pan if sauce becomes too thick.

Nutritional Data

PER SERVING:

Calories:	25.7
Fat (gm):	13.1
Sat. fat (gm):	3.1
Cholesterol (mg):	38.2
Sodium (mg):	244
% Calories from fat:	33

EXCHANGES:

Milk:	0.0	Bread:	0.6
Veg.:	0.4	Meat:	2.1
Fruit:	0.0	Fat:	1.6

Thick and Hearty Mushroom Sauce

Yield 3 cups *(6 half-cup servings)*

- 1 cup white wine
- 1½ tablespoons cornstarch
- 1 lb. mushrooms, thinly sliced
- ¼ cup onion, diced
- 1 clove garlic, minced
- 2 cups defatted chicken stock
- 1 tablespoon Italian seasoning
- Salt and pepper to taste

Dissolve cornstarch in wine. Combine remaining ingredients, except salt and pepper, and bring to boil. Reduce heat and simmer 3-4 minutes. Thicken with cornstarch and wine mixture, stirring constantly. Simmer gently another 3-5 minutes. Season with salt and pepper.

Nutritional Data

PER SERVING:		EXCHANGES:	
Calories:	69	Milk:	0.0
Fat (gm):	0.8	Vegetable:	0.8
Sat. fat (gm):	0.2	Fruit:	0.0
Cholesterol (mg):	0	Bread:	0.1
Sodium (mg):	264	Meat:	0.0
% Calories from fat:	10	Fat:	0.6

EASY BEEF AND NOODLES
with Thick and Hearty Mushroom Sauce

Serves 6
Non-stick cooking spray
2 tablespoons canola oil
1 lb. beef cubes (round steak)
3 cups *Thick and Hearty Mushroom Sauce*
4 cups cooked wide noodles
Salt and pepper to taste

Coat skillet with non-stick spray. Heat oil until barely smoking. Brown beef cubes on all sides. In saucepan, combine browned cubes and Thick and Hearty Mushroom Sauce. Simmer 30 minutes. Add water if sauce becomes too thick. Season with salt and pepper, and serve with cooked noodles.

Nutritional Data
PER SERVING:

Calories:	377		
Fat (gm):	14.1		
Sat. fat (gm):	4		
Cholesterol (mg):	50.9		
Sodium (mg):	340		
% Calories from fat:	30		

EXCHANGES:

Milk:	0.0	Bread:	1.7
Veg.:	0.8	Meat:	2.8
Fruit:	0.0	Fat:	1.8

CHICKEN BREASTS IN PACKETS
with Thick and Hearty Mushroom Sauce

Serves 6
6 boneless chicken breasts, skin removed
6 squares of foil, 12x12 inches
3 cups *Thick and Hearty Mushroom Sauce*

Preheat oven to 375 degrees. Fold each foil square in half. Open the fold and place a chicken breast on lower half of foil. Top each chicken breast with ½ cup Thick and Hearty Mushroom Sauce.

Fold top half of foil over chicken and sauce. Crimp edges to prevent leaking. Bake in 375-degree oven 20 minutes. Serve with foil square still closed, and allow each person to open their own.

Nutritional Data
PER SERVING:

Calories:	193		
Fat (gm):	2.2		
Sat. fat (gm):	0.6		
Cholesterol (mg):	65.7		
Sodium (mg):	338		
% Calories from fat:	10		

EXCHANGES:

Milk:	0.0	Bread:	1.1
Veg.:	0.8	Meat:	2.9
Fruit:	0.0	Fat:	0.6

LIGHT TARTAR SAUCE

Yield 3 cups *(12 quarter-cup servings)*

  2 cups non-fat mayonnaise
 ¼ cup onion, diced
 ¼ cup capers, chopped
 ¼ cup low-salt pickle, chopped
  2 tablespoons fresh parsley, minced
  1 tablespoon fresh lemon juice
  1 teaspoon sugar
     Dash chili sauce, *or* Tabasco

ombine ingredients and let refrigerate at least 1 hour before using.

Nutritional Data

PER SERVING:		EXCHANGES:	
Calories:	32	Milk:	0.0
Fat (gm):	trace	Vegetable:	0.1
Sat. fat (gm):	trace	Fruit:	0.5
Cholesterol (mg):	0	Bread:	0.0
Sodium (mg):	430	Meat:	0.0
% Calories from fat:	1	Fat:	0.0

OVEN "FRIED" CATFISH
with Light Tartar Sauce

Serves 6

1 cup cornmeal
1 teaspoon cayenne
1 tablespoon dried thyme, crumbled
6 large catfish fillets
Non-stick cooking spray
2 cups *Light Tartar Sauce*

Preheat oven to 400 degrees. Combine cornmeal, thyme, and cayenne. Dredge fillets in seasoned cornmeal and shake off excess. Place fillets on non-stick baking sheet, and spray fish lightly with non-stick spray. Bake in 400-degree oven until crispy and golden, 20-25 minutes. Serve hot with cold Light Tartar Sauce.

Nutritional Data

PER SERVING:

Calories:	167
Fat (gm):	2.3
Sat. fat (gm):	0.7
Cholesterol (mg):	40
Sodium (mg):	792
% Calories from fat:	12

EXCHANGES:

Milk:	0.0	Bread:	0.8
Veg.:	0.2	Meat:	1.5
Fruit:	1.0	Fat:	0.0

TUNA BURGERS
with Light Tartar Sauce

Serves 6

1 lb. canned, water-pack, low-sodium tuna, drained
¼ cup onion minced
¼ cup olives minced
1 clove garlic, minced
2 egg whites
½ cup breadcrumbs
1 tablespoon dried basil
3 tablespoons canola oil
3 cups *Light Tartar Sauce*

Combine all ingredients, except oil and Light Tartar Sauce, and form into 6 patties. Heat oil in non-stick skillet until barely smoking. Brown patties, cooking 2-3 minutes per side. Top each patty with low-fat cheese, optional if desired. Serve on reduced-calorie roll (not included in nutritional data) with lettuce and Light Tartar Sauce.

Nutritional Data

PER SERVING:

Calories:	204
Fat (gm):	2.1
Sat. fat (gm):	0.4
Cholesterol (mg):	22.7
Sodium (mg):	781
% Calories from fat:	10

EXCHANGES:

Milk:	0.0	Bread:	0.4
Veg.:	0.3	Meat:	1.7
Fruit:	1.0	Fat:	0.2

Savory Raisin Sauce

Yield 3 cups *(6 half-cup servings)*

1 tablespoon cornstarch dissolved in ¼ cup port wine
2 cups defatted chicken stock
1 clove garlic
¼ cup onion, minced
½ cup raisins

Over medium heat, thicken cornstarch in port wine mixture, stirring constantly. Add stock, onion, and garlic and bring to boil. Reduce heat and simmer 2-3 minutes. Add raisins.

Nutritional Data

PER SERVING:		EXCHANGES:	
Calories:	70	Milk:	0.0
Fat (gm):	0.5	Vegetable:	0.1
Sat. fat (gm):	0.2	Fruit:	0.7
Cholesterol (mg):	0	Bread:	0.1
Sodium (mg):	261	Meat:	0.0
% Calories from fat:	7	Fat:	0.1

GLAZED BONELESS HAM
with Savory Raisin Sauce

Serves 6

1 boneless light ham, approximately 2½-3
  lbs., heated according to package directions
  Light Glaze (see recipe below)
2 cups *Savory Raisin Sauce*

Light Glaze

¼ cup prepared mustard
¼ cup warm water
2 tablespoons brown sugar
2 tablespoons honey
2 tablespoons red wine vinegar

Nutritional Data
PER SERVING:

Calories:	310
Fat (gm):	9
Sat. fat (gm):	2.7
Cholesterol (mg):	70.9
Sodium (mg):	799
% Calories from fat:	25

EXCHANGES:

Milk:	0.0	Bread:	0.1
Veg.:	0.4	Meat:	3.5
Fruit:	1.2	Fat:	0.3

Combine ingredients for Light Glaze until thoroughly dissolved. Half an hour before ham is done, glaze liberally. Slice and serve with Savory Raisin Sauce.

APPLES STUFFED WITH CHICKEN AND VEAL "SAUSAGE"

Serves 6

Light Sausage (see recipe below)
3 extra-large apples
3 cups *Savory Raisin Sauce*

Light Sausage

¾ lb. ground chicken
¾ lb. ground veal
1 clove garlic
¼ cup onion, minced
2 tablespoons low-sodium ketchup
2 tablespoons bourbon
1 tablespoon dried thyme
1 tablespoon fennel seed

Nutritional Data
PER SERVING:

Calories:	350
Fat (gm):	11.4
Sat. fat (gm):	4.2
Cholesterol (mg):	99.8
Sodium (mg):	406
% Calories from fat:	29

EXCHANGES:

Milk:	0.0	Bread:	0.1
Veg.:	0.2	Meat:	3.8
Fruit:	1.5	Fat:	0.9

Combine all ingredients for "sausage" mixture. Cut apples in halves. Scoop out apple flesh with melon ball cutter. Fill and mound sausage mixture inside scooped out apple halves.

Place in baking dish. Pour Savory Raisin Sauce over stuffed apples. Bake at 350 degrees about 45 minutes until done.

LEMON ARTICHOKE SAUCE

Yield 3 cups *(6 half-cup servings)*

1 cup defatted chicken stock
1 can artichokes, drained
1 large clove garlic, minced
½ cup fresh lemon juice
   Zest of 1 lemon
½ cup non-fat sour cream
   Salt and pepper to taste

Add artichokes and garlic to stock and bring to boil. Reduce heat and simmer 5 minutes. Add lemon juice and zest. Puree in food processor or blender. Stir in sour cream and heat through but do not boil. Season with salt and pepper.

Nutritional Data

PER SERVING:		EXCHANGES:	
Calories:	45	Milk:	0.2
Fat (gm):	0.3	Vegetable:	0.8
Sat. fat (gm):	0.1	Fruit:	0.1
Cholesterol (mg):	0	Bread:	0.0
Sodium (mg):	174	Meat:	0.0
% Calories from fat:	6	Fat:	0.0

GRILLED DIJON LAMB CHOPS
with Lemon Artichoke Sauce

Serves 6

12 extra-lean lamb loin chops
1 cup Dijon mustard
1 cup molasses
3 cups *Lemon Artichoke Sauce*

Combine mustard and molasses. Bring to boil. Chill thoroughly. Coat lamb chops with mustard sauce, and marinate 30 minutes or more. Grill chops over hot coals 2-3 minutes per side for medium-rare. Serve with Lemon Artichoke Sauce.

Nutritional Data

PER SERVING:

Calories:	421
Fat (gm):	11.3
Sat. fat (gm):	3.4
Cholesterol (mg):	87.4
Sodium (mg):	793
% Calories from fat:	24

EXCHANGES:

Milk:	0.2	Bread:	0.0
Veg.:	1.5	Meat:	3.3
Fruit:	2.8	Fat:	0.3

PORK MEDALLIONS IN SHERRY
with Lemon Artichoke Sauce

Serves 6

2 tablespoons canola oil
1½ lbs. extra-lean pork, cut into medallions
1 cup defatted chicken stock
½ cup sherry
2 cups *Lemon Artichoke Sauce*

Heat oil in non-stick skillet until barely smoking. Brown pork medallions on both sides. Add stock and sherry and simmer until tender, 30-45 minutes.

Stir often and let liquid almost evaporate by the time pork is done. Add 2 cups Lemon Artichoke Sauce and heat through. Do not boil. Serve with rice or pasta.

Nutritional Data

PER SERVING:

Calories:	356
Fat (gm):	14
Sat. fat (gm):	5.9
Cholesterol (mg):	89.4
Sodium (mg):	357
% Calories from fat:	30

EXCHANGES:

Milk:	0.2	Bread:	0.0
Veg.:	0.8	Meat:	4.0
Fruit:	0.1	Fat:	1.4

APPLE-SHALLOT SAUCE

Yield 3 cups *(12 quarter-cup servings)*

1 cup apple jelly
1 cup apple juice
2 tablespoons apple cider vinegar
2 tablespoons shallots, minced
2 large garlic cloves, minced
2 tablespoons low-sodium soy sauce
1 large Granny Smith apple, peeled and sliced

ombine all ingredients and bring to boil. Reduce heat and simmer 5 minutes.

Nutritional Data

PER SERVING:		EXCHANGES:	
Calories:	65	Milk:	0.0
Fat (gm):	trace	Vegetable:	0.1
Sat. fat (gm):	trace	Fruit:	1.5
Cholesterol (mg):	0	Bread:	0.0
Sodium (mg):	137	Meat:	0.0
% Calories from fat:	1	Fat:	0.0

ROASTED CORNISH GAME HENS
with Apple-Shallot Sauce

Serves 6

6 large Cornish game hens
Marinade (see recipe below)
2½ cups *Apple Shallot Sauce*, divided

Marinade

2 cups apple cider
2 large cloves garlic, crushed
1 tablespoon dried thyme
1 cup white wine

Nutritional Data

PER SERVING:

Calories:	311
Fat (gm):	9
Sat. fat (gm):	2.6
Cholesterol (mg):	89
Sodium (mg):	532
% Calories from fat:	26

EXCHANGES:

Milk:	0.0	Bread:	0.0
Veg.:	0.1	Meat:	4.3
Fruit:	1.4	Fat:	0.3

Combine ingredients for Marinade. Marinate hens 1 hour or overnight. Roast in 350-degree oven 1 hour. Baste every 15 minutes, using 2 cups Apple-Shallot Sauce. Cut each game hen in half. Serve remaining Apple-Shallot Sauce warm as accompaniment.

SHRIMP AND APPLE RUMAKI
with Apple-Shallot Sauce

Serves 15 *(approximately 2 per serving)*

1 lb. fresh shrimp, peeled and deveined
1½ cups apple slices
30 strips of turkey bacon, *or* vegetarian bacon
Toothpicks
3 cups *Apple Shallot Sauce*

Nutritional Data

PER SERVING:

Calories:	140
Fat (gm):	5.4
Sat. fat (gm):	0.9
Cholesterol (mg):	46
Sodium (mg):	388
% Calories from fat:	30

EXCHANGES:

Milk:	0.0	Bread:	0.0
Veg.:	0.2	Meat:	1.1
Fruit:	1.0	Fat:	0.8

Wrap together 1 shrimp and 1 apple slice with strip of turkey bacon. Secure with toothpick. Spoon Apple Shallot Sauce over each bacon-wrapped rumaki.

Broil until bacon is crisp and shrimp is cooked, 3-5 minutes. Serve with individual bowls of Apple-Shallot Sauce for dipping.

10.
DESSERT SAUCES

Raspberry Sauce

Brown Sugar Banana Sauce

Vanilla Rum Sauce

Heavenly Mango Sauce

Coffee-Brandy Sauce

Light Lemon Sour Cream Sauce

Spiced Peach Sauce

RASPBERRY SAUCE

Yield 2 cups (8 quarter-cup servings)
1 pkg. frozen raspberries
½ cup sugar
  Sugar Twin brown sugar substitute equivalent
  to ½ cup brown sugar
  Juice and zest of 1 lemon
2 tablespoons fruit-flavored brandy

P uree raspberries and strain out seeds through fine strainer or cheesecloth. Add sugar, sugar substitute, lemon juice, zest, and brandy. Refrigerate at least 1 hour before serving.

Nutritional Data

PER SERVING:		EXCHANGES:	
Calories:	81	Milk:	0.0
Fat (gm):	0.2	Vegetable:	0.0
Sat. fat (gm):	trace	Fruit:	1.2
Cholesterol (mg):	0	Bread:	0.0
Sodium (mg):	trace	Meat:	0.0
% Calories from fat:	1	Fat:	0.3

APRICOT BLINTZES
with Raspberry Sauce

Serves 8 (1 crepe per serving)

Crepes

8 egg whites
1 cup skim milk
½ teaspoon salt
1¼ cups flour
3 tablespoons canola oil
3 cups *Raspberry Sauce*

Filling

1½ lbs. low-fat ricotta cheese
2 egg whites
1 cup reduced-calorie apricot preserves

Nutritional Data

PER SERVING:

Calories:	398
Fat (gm):	12.3
Sat. fat (gm):	4.6
Cholesterol (mg):	26.8
Sodium (mg):	338
% Calories from fat:	28

EXCHANGES:

Milk:	0.1	Bread:	0.8
Veg.:	0.0	Meat:	2.0
Fruit:	2.2	Fat:	2.1

Preheat oven to 350 degrees. Combine all ingredients for Crepes, except oil and Raspberry Sauce, and chill 1 hour.

Combine Filling ingredients and mix until smooth.

Heat a little canola oil in non-stick skillet. Pour in enough batter to make 1 thin crepe. Cook each crepe on only one side.

When all crepes are made, place 1½ tablespoons Filling in center of each. Fold sides in to enclose filling. Heat in oven 15-20 minutes. Serve warm with Raspberry Sauce.

OLD-FASHIONED BREAD PUDDING
with Raspberry Sauce

Serves 6

2 tablespoons cinnamon

1 teaspoon nutmeg

2 cups skim milk

4 egg whites

½ cup raisins

¼ cup rum

½ cup white sugar
  Sugar Twin brown sugar substitute equivalent to ½ cup brown sugar

6 slices stale, reduced-calorie white bread, cubed

3 cups *Raspberry Sauce*

Nutritional Data

PER SERVING:

Calories:	321
Fat (gm):	1
Sat. fat (gm):	0.2
Cholesterol (mg):	1.5
Sodium (mg):	191
% Calories from fat:	3

EXCHANGES:

Milk:	0.3	Bread:	0.5
Veg.:	0.0	Meat:	0.3
Fruit:	3.3	Fat:	0.9

Preheat oven to 350 degrees. Mix all ingredients, except bread cubes and Raspberry Sauce, thoroughly. Place bread cubes in 8x8-inch casserole or baking dish, and pour batter over all. Let stand at least 15 minutes until batter is fully absorbed. Bake 1 hour at 350 degrees. Serve with Raspberry Sauce.

BROWN SUGAR BANANA SAUCE

Yield 2 cups *(4 half-cup servings)*

½ cup brown sugar
 Sugar Twin brown sugar substitute equivalent
 to ½ cup brown sugar
½ cup water
 2 large bananas, sliced
 1 tablespoon cinnamon
¼ cup rum

C ombine brown sugar, sugar substitute, and water. Bring to boil to make a thick syrup. Add bananas, cinnamon, and rum. Bring to boil again. Serve warm.

Nutritional Data

PER SERVING:		EXCHANGES:	
Calories:	61	Milk:	0.0
Fat (gm):	2.7	Vegetable:	0.0
Sat. fat (gm):	0.1	Fruit:	2.0
Cholesterol (mg):	0	Bread:	0.0
Sodium (mg):	22	Meat:	0.0
% Calories from fat:	1	Fat:	0.8

LOW-FAT BANANAS FOSTER

Serves 6

¼ cup rum (preferably 151 proof)
2 cups *Brown Sugar Banana Sauce*
1 qt. frozen non-fat vanilla yogurt

Nutritional Data

PER SERVING:

Calories:	264
Fat (gm):	1.9
Sat. fat (gm):	1.2
Cholesterol (mg):	6.8
Sodium (mg):	94
% Calories from fat:	6

EXCHANGES:

Milk:	0.6	Bread:	0.0
Veg.:	0.0	Meat:	0.0
Fruit:	2.4	Fat:	1.3

Exercising *extreme caution,* gently heat but do not boil rum. Add heated rum to hot Brown Sugar Banana Sauce. Being very careful to avert your face, ignite sauce with long kitchen match. Do not use regular matches since there is not enough margin for safety!

Rum and sauce mixture should ignite and burn about 1 minute. Stir while sauce is still flaming, and serve immediately over frozen vanilla yogurt.

BANANA FRITTERS
with Brown Sugar Banana Sauce

Serves 6

1 tablespoon sugar
1 tablespoon dry yeast
1 cup lukewarm skim milk
2 cups banana pulp and chunks
  Juice and zest of 1 lemon
4 egg whites
1¼ cups flour
3 tablespoons canola oil
2 cups *Brown Sugar Banana Sauce*

Nutritional Data

PER SERVING:

Calories:	371
Fat (gm):	7.8
Sat. fat (gm):	0.8
Cholesterol (mg):	0.7
Sodium (mg):	74
% Calories from fat:	18

EXCHANGES:

Milk:	0.2	Bread:	1.2
Veg.:	0.1	Meat:	0.3
Fruit:	2.7	Fat:	1.9

Dissolve sugar and yeast in lukewarm milk, and let yeast proof 5 minutes. Toss bananas with lemon juice and zest. Add egg whites and yeast mixture. Stir in flour, and let rise 30 minutes to 1 hour.

Spoon ⅙ of batter onto oiled non-stick skillet or griddle. Cook over low heat until both sides of fritter are browned, flipping once. Serve fritters hot with warm Brown Sugar Banana Sauce.

VANILLA RUM SAUCE

Yield 3 cups (6 half-cup servings)

2 cups water
½ cup white sugar
Sugar substitute equivalent to ½ cup sugar
½ cup brown sugar
Sugar Twin brown sugar substitute equivalent
to ½ cup brown sugar
1 tablespoon cornstarch dissolved in ¼ cup rum
1 tablespoon vanilla extract
1 tablespoon molasses

C ombine water, white sugar, brown sugar, and sugar substitutes. Bring to boil and thicken with cornstarch and rum mixture. Add vanilla and molasses. Chill at least 1 hour before serving.

Nutritional Data

PER SERVING:		EXCHANGES:	
Calories:	59	Milk:	0.0
Fat (gm):	trace	Vegetable:	0.0
Sat. fat (gm):	0	Fruit:	2.1
Cholesterol (mg):	0	Bread:	0.1
Sodium (mg):	16	Meat:	0.0
% Calories from fat:	1	Fat:	0.6

POACHED PEARS
in Vanilla Rum Sauce

Serves 6

3 cups *Vanilla Rum Sauce*
1 cinnamon stick, *or* 1 tablespoon ground cinnamon
6 pears (Anjou or Bartlett)
  Juice of 1 lemon

Nutritional Data

PER SERVING:

Calories:	259
Fat (gm):	0.7
Sat. fat (gm):	trace
Cholesterol (mg):	0
Sodium (mg):	16
% Calories from fat:	2

EXCHANGES:

Milk:	0.0	Bread:	0.1
Veg.:	0.0	Meat:	0.0
Fruit:	3.8	Fat:	0.6

Bring Vanilla Rum Sauce and cinnamon stick to boil. Remove cinnamon stick and reduce heat. Peel pears, remove seeds, quarter, and combine with lemon juice. Add pears to sauce, and simmer over very low heat 30 minutes or until soft. Cooking time will depend on firmness of pears. Cool pears in their own syrup and refrigerate.

BANANA CHERRY BREAD
with Vanilla Rum Sauce

Serves 6

Non-stick cooking spray
4 egg whites
⅓ cup brown sugar, firmly packed
  Sugar Twin brown sugar substitute equivalent to ⅓ cup brown sugar
⅓ cup applesauce
1 cup bananas, mashed
1½ teaspoons low-sodium baking powder
½ teaspoon baking soda
½ teaspoon salt
1¾ cups flour
1 cup tart dried cherries
3 cups *Vanilla Rum Sauce*

Nutritional Data

PER SERVING:

Calories:	379
Fat (gm):	0.7
Sat. fat (gm):	0.2
Cholesterol (mg):	0
Sodium (mg):	310
% Calories from fat:	2

EXCHANGES:

Milk:	0.0	Bread:	1.6
Veg.:	0.0	Meat:	0.3
Fruit:	3.4	Fat:	0.7

Preheat oven to 350 degrees. Prepare loaf pan with non-stick cooking spray.

Thoroughly mix egg whites, sugar, sugar substitute, applesauce, and bananas. Separately, mix baking powder, baking soda, salt, and flour. Combine wet and dry ingredients, and mix completely.

Fold in dried cherries. Pour batter into prepared pan. Bake approximately 45-50 minutes or until knife inserted in center comes out clean. Serve each slice on pool of Vanilla Rum Sauce.

HEAVENLY MANGO SAUCE

Yield 3 cups *(12 quarter-cup servings)*

2 cups apricot nectar
1 ripe mango, *or* 1 cup canned mango slices
  Zest and juice of 1 lime
¼ cup honey
¼ cup fresh mint, chopped (optional)

 ombine first 4 ingredients, and puree in food processor or blender. Stir in mint if available. Chill 1 hour before using.

Nutritional Data

PER SERVING:		EXCHANGES:	
Calories:	67	Milk:	0.0
Fat (gm):	0.1	Vegetable:	0.0
Sat. fat (gm):	trace	Fruit:	1.5
Cholesterol (mg):	0	Bread:	0.0
Sodium (mg):	2	Meat:	0.0
% Calories from fat:	1	Fat:	0.0

MANGO COBBLER
with Heavenly Mango Sauce

Serves 6

1 tablespoon cornstarch dissolved in ¼ cup apple juice, *or* white grape juice

1 tablespoon cinnamon

¼ cup sugar

¼ cup honey

1 egg white

1 large ripe mango, peeled and flesh cut away from pit

Cobbler Batter (see recipe below)

3 cups *Heavenly Mango Sauce*

Cobbler Batter

1¼ cups flour

¼ cup white sugar

Sugar Twin brown sugar substitute equivalent to ¼ cup brown sugar

1 teaspoon low-sodium baking powder

½ teaspoon baking soda

2 egg whites

¼ cup skim milk

Nutritional Data

PER SERVING:

Calories:	376
Fat (gm):	0.6
Sat. fat (gm):	0.1
Cholesterol (mg):	0.2
Sodium (mg):	45
% Calories from fat:	1

EXCHANGES:

Milk:	0.0	Bread:	1.2
Veg.:	0.0	Meat:	0.3
Fruit:	4.3	Fat:	0.0

Preheat oven to 375 degrees. To cornstarch and juice mixture, add cinnamon, sugar, honey and egg white. Stir in mango, and pour into baking dish.

To make Cobbler Batter, combine all dry ingredients in bowl; combine egg whites and milk in another. Stir contents of both bowls together.

Pour Cobbler Batter over fruit mixture, and bake in 375-degree oven about 30 minutes. Serve with Heavenly Mango Sauce.

PEAR CLOUDS
with Heavenly Mango Sauce

Serves 6

6 pears
¼ cup fresh lemon juice
¼ cup sugar
8 egg whites
Pinch of salt
3 cups *Heavenly Mango Sauce*

Peel and core pears, and toss with lemon juice and sugar. Let pears stand ½ hour. Bake in 350-degree oven about 20 minutes, *or* on high in microwave oven 3-5 minutes. Pears should be soft but still firm enough to hold their shape.

Add salt to egg whites and whip until stiff peaks form, but do not let them dry out. Using pastry bag, pipe meringue around pears, totally encasing them.

Slow bake meringue-surrounded pears in 275-degree oven 1-1½ hours until meringue is dried out. Serve with Heavenly Mango Sauce.

Nutritional Data

PER SERVING:

Calories:	288
Fat (gm):	0.9
Sat. fat (gm):	0.1
Cholesterol (mg):	0
Sodium (mg):	78
% Calories from fat:	3

EXCHANGES:

Milk:	0.0	Bread:	0.0
Veg.:	0.0	Meat:	0.7
Fruit:	4.3	Fat:	0.0

COFFEE-BRANDY SAUCE

Yield 2 cups *(8 quarter-cup servings)*

2 cups water
1 cup sugar
  Sugar Twin brown sugar substitute equivalent
  to 1 cup brown sugar
1 tablespoon cornstarch dissolved in ¼ cup
  brandy
2 tablespoons instant coffee (liquid form),
  regular or decaf
1 tablespoon vanilla extract

C ombine water, sugar, and brown sugar substitute and bring to boil. Thicken with cornstarch and brandy mixture, stirring constantly. Remove from heat, and add coffee and vanilla extract. Chill 1 hour before serving.

Nutritional Data

PER SERVING:		EXCHANGES:	
Calories:	87	Milk:	0.0
Fat (gm):	trace	Vegetable:	0.0
Sat. fat (gm):	0	Fruit:	1.1
Cholesterol (mg):	0	Bread:	0.1
Sodium (mg):	10	Meat:	0.0
% Calories from fat:	1	Fat:	0.4

COFFEE-BRANDY FROZEN YOGURT

Serves 6

2 8-oz. containers non-fat coffee yogurt
1 8-oz. container non-fat vanilla yogurt
½ cup skim milk
1 tablespoon instant coffee (liquid form), regular or decaf
2 tablespoons brandy
1 egg white
2 cups *Coffee-Brandy Sauce*

Combine all ingredients, and freeze in ice cream freezer according to manufacturer's instructions. Serve with hot Coffee-Brandy Sauce.

Nutritional Data

PER SERVING:

Calories:	258
Fat (gm):	0.2
Sat. fat (gm):	0.2
Cholesterol (mg):	2.4
Sodium (mg):	126
% Calories from fat:	1

EXCHANGES:

Milk:	0.8	Bread:	0.1
Veg.:	0.0	Meat:	0.1
Fruit:	2.2	Fat:	1.0

JEWISH HONEY CAKE
with Coffee-Brandy Sauce

Serves 14 (1 slice per serving)

¾ cup very strong coffee, regular or decaf
2 cups honey
¼ cup molasses
¼ cup brandy
8 egg whites
4 tablespoons coffee-flavored yogurt
½ cup dark brown sugar
  Sugar Twin brown sugar substitute equivalent to ½ cup brown sugar
3½ cups sifted flour
3 teaspoons low-sodium baking powder
1 teaspoon baking soda
½ teaspoon each of cinnamon, ground clove, nutmeg, and ground ginger
  Non-stick cooking spray
2 cups *Coffee-Brandy Sauce*

Nutritional Data

PER SERVING:

Calories:	394
Fat (gm):	0.3
Sat. fat (gm):	0.1
Cholesterol (mg):	0.3
Sodium (mg):	123
% Calories from fat:	1

EXCHANGES:

Milk:	0.1	Bread:	1.3
Veg.:	0.0	Meat:	0.3
Fruit:	3.9	Fat:	0.5

Preheat oven to 300 degrees. Combine coffee, honey, and molasses in saucepan and bring to boil. Let mixture cool and add brandy.

Beat yogurt and brown sugar into egg whites.

In separate bowl, sift flour, baking powder, baking soda, and spices together. Alternately stir flour and honey mixture into egg white mixture. Pour batter into two 9x5-inch loaf pans sprayed with non-stick cooking spray.

Bake 70 minutes or until cake surface springs back to the touch. When cakes are done, brush with Coffee-Brandy Sauce and leave out overnight. Serve with remaining Coffee-Brandy Sauce as accompaniment.

LIGHT LEMON SOUR CREAM SAUCE

Yield 3 cups (12 quarter-cup servings)

8 ozs. non-fat sour cream
8 ozs. non-fat cream cheese
8 ozs. non-fat whipped topping
Zest and juice of 1 lemon
½ cup brown sugar
Sugar Twin brown sugar substitute equivalent
to ½ cup brown sugar

Thoroughly blend sour cream and cream cheese. Into whipped topping, fold lemon juice, zest, brown sugar and sugar substitute. Combine all ingredients, and gently fold together.

Nutritional Data

PER SERVING:		EXCHANGES:	
Calories:	108	Milk:	0.3
Fat (gm):	6.2	Vegetable:	0.0
Sat. fat (gm):	5.2	Fruit:	0.6
Cholesterol (mg):	10.5	Bread:	0.1
Sodium (mg):	87	Meat:	0.2
% Calories from fat:	15	Fat:	1.6

TRIPLE APPLE CAKE
with Light Lemon Sour Cream Sauce

Serves 10

Non-stick cooking spray
2 cups unbleached flour
¼ cup white sugar
⅛ cup brown sugar
Sugar Twin brown sugar substitute equivalent to ⅛ cup brown sugar
1 tablespoon ground cinnamon
1 teaspoon baking soda
1 teaspoon low-sodium baking powder
4 egg whites
½ cup non-fat plain yogurt
½ cup applesauce
2 apples, roughly chopped
1 teaspoon vanilla extract
¼ cup apple jelly
3 cups *Light Lemon Sour Cream Sauce*

Nutritional Data

PER SERVING:

Calories:	332
Fat (gm):	10.1
Sat. fat (gm):	7.5
Cholesterol (mg):	12.9
Sodium (mg):	214
% Calories from fat:	27

EXCHANGES:

Milk:	0.4	Bread:	1.1
Veg.:	0.0	Meat:	0.4
Fruit:	1.8	Fat:	1.9

Preheat oven to 375 degrees. Prepare 9-inch bundt pan with non-stick cooking spray.

In large bowl, mix flour, both types of sugar, sugar substitute, cinnamon, baking soda, and baking powder. In another bowl, combine egg whites, yogurt, applesauce, apples, and vanilla extract. Mix contents of both bowls together.

Pour batter into prepared pan. Bake at 375 degrees 25-30 minutes. Let stand 5 minutes before unmolding. When cake is cool, melt apple jelly and brush on top and sides. Serve with Light Lemon Sour Cream Sauce.

LIGHT LEMON SOUR CREAM PAVLOVA

Serves 6

6 egg whites
1 cup sugar
   Sugar Twin brown sugar substitute equivalent to 1 cup brown sugar
   Pinch of salt
1 teaspoon vanilla extract
1 teaspoon lemon juice
   Zest of 1 lemon
   Non-stick cooking spray
2 cups *Light Lemon Sour Cream Sauce*
2 cups combined strawberries and blueberries

Nutritional Data

PER SERVING:

Calories:	276
Fat (gm):	9.9
Sat. fat (gm):	7.5
Cholesterol (mg):	12.7
Sodium (mg):	142
% Calories from fat:	31

EXCHANGES:

Milk:	0.3	Bread:	0.1
Veg.:	0.0	Meat:	0.5
Fruit:	2.2	Fat:	2.0

Beat egg whites until soft peaks begin to form. Gradually beat in sugar, sugar substitute, salt, vanilla extract, and lemon juice. When meringue is stiff, gently and quickly fold in zest.

Pour into a 10-inch springform pan prepared with non-stick spray. Make a well in center of meringue mixture. Bake at 275 degrees 1-1½ hours (meringue actually dries out rather than bakes).

Remove from oven and fill meringue shell with Light Lemon Sour Cream Sauce. Top generously with fresh berries.

SPICED PEACH SAUCE

Yield 2 cups (4 half-cup servings)

1 can peaches in light syrup
1 tablespoon cinnamon
¼ teaspoon nutmeg
2 tablespoons peach brandy
1 tablespoon vanilla extract

ombine all ingredients and puree in food processor or blender. Chill at least 1 hour before serving.

Nutritional Data

PER SERVING:		EXCHANGES:	
Calories:	65	Milk:	0.0
Fat (gm):	trace	Vegetable:	0.0
Sat. fat (gm):	trace	Fruit:	0.6
Cholesterol (mg):	0	Bread:	0.0
Sodium (mg):	4	Meat:	0.0
% Calories from fat:	1	Fat:	0.5

PEACH CRISP WITH ALMOND TOPPING
with Spiced Peach Sauce

Serves 6

- 6 cups peach slices
- Juice of 1 lemon
- 1/8 cup brown sugar
- Sugar Twin brown sugar substitute equivalent to 1/8 cup brown sugar
- 1/4 cup honey
- 1 tablespoon cornstarch
- 2 tablespoons cinnamon
- 1 teaspoon almond extract
- Topping (see recipe below)
- Non-stick cooking spray
- 2 cups *Spiced Peach Sauce*

Topping

- 1½ cups rolled oats
- 3/4 cup flour
- 1/4 cup brown sugar
- 1 teaspoon cinnamon
- 1/4 cup almonds, sliced

Nutritional Data

PER SERVING:

Calories:	347
Fat (gm):	3.6
Sat. fat (gm):	0.5
Cholesterol (mg):	0
Sodium (mg):	12
% Calories from fat:	9

EXCHANGES:

Milk:	0.0	Bread:	1.4
Veg.:	0.0	Meat:	0.1
Fruit:	5.5	Fat:	0.7

Thoroughly combine all ingredients except Topping, non-stick spray, and Spiced Peach Sauce. Let mixture stand ½ hour to create its own juice.

Mix ingredients for Topping together in separate bowl. Prepare 9x13-inch baking dish with non-stick spray. Pour in peach mixture, and place Topping evenly across surface. Spray lightly with non-stick cooking spray.

Bake in 350-degree oven about 45 minutes until peaches are bubbly and Topping is browned. Serve warm with Spiced Peach Sauce.

GINGERBREAD DESSERT
with Spiced Peach Sauce

Serves 6

Non-stick cooking spray
2 egg whites
¾ cup plain non-fat yogurt
½ cup applesauce
¼ cup brown sugar
Sugar Twin brown sugar substitute equivalent to ¼ cup brown sugar
¾ cup molasses
2 cups sifted flour
½ teaspoon salt
½ teaspoon baking soda
1½ teaspoons low-sodium baking powder
1½ teaspoons ground ginger
1 teaspoon cinnamon
¼ teaspoon cloves, ground
2 cups *Spiced Peach Sauce*

Nutritional Data

PER SERVING:

Calories:	350
Fat (gm):	0.5
Sat. fat (gm):	0.1
Cholesterol (mg):	0.6
Sodium (mg):	315
% Calories from fat:	1

EXCHANGES:

Milk:	0.2	Bread:	1.7
Veg.:	0.0	Meat:	0.2
Fruit:	3.0	Fat:	0.4

Preheat oven to 350 degrees. Prepare 8x8x2-inch loaf pan with non-stick spray.

Whip together egg whites, yogurt, and applesauce. Add brown sugar, sugar substitute, and molasses. Sift together flour, salt, baking soda, baking powder, and spices.

Stir dry ingredients into wet ingredients, and stir only until mixed. Pour into prepared pan, and bake about 45 minutes. Serve with Spiced Peach Sauce.

11.
SAUCERY BY MAIL

American Spoon Foods
P.O. Box 566
1668 Clarion Avenue
Petoskey, MI 49770-0566
(800) 222-5886
(616) 347-9030

Specialties of the house here are low-sugar jams and preserves in luscious flavors like Blueberry Lime and Cherry Gooseberry. Also unusual tangy condiments like Cranberry Catsup and Plum Catsup. A great source for the complete line of Chef Larry Forgione's sumptuous sauces, including Peanut, Southwestern-style Adobo, and zippy Barbecue.

The Chef's Pantry
P.O. Box 3
Post Mills, VT 05058
(800) 666-9940
(802) 333-4141

A wonderful resource for unusual mustards including black olive, lime, shallot, and chervil flavors. Chef's Pantry imports from a wide variety of producers, mostly French.

Putney's Specialty Foods
2415 S.E. 10th Street
Portland, OR 97214
(800) 627-0657
(503) 236-1169

Putney rhymes with chutney, which is the specialty of the house here. What is chutney? Imagine sweet and sour preserves with not too much sugar, and you've got the right idea. My favorite Putney chutney (try saying that five times fast!) is Spicy Carrot Lemon, which is great when spread on low-calorie turkey sandwiches. Other flavors include Cranberry-Tangerine and Apple Walnut.

Blanchard & Blanchard
P.O. Box 1080
Norwich, VT 05055
(802) 295-9200

Their Sesame Seed Salad Dressing is addictive, and they also offer a full line of marinades. Their no-oil dressings can make eating salad an infinitely more pleasant prospect if you're trying to lose weight.

Balducci's
Mail Order Division
11-02 Queens Plaza South
Long Island City, NY 11101-4908
(800) 822-1444
(800) 247-2450 (in NY state)

This is the reigning king of pasta sauce purveyors. These rich but skinny sauces are packed with ingredients like fresh basil, walnuts, and mushrooms.

Kitchen Kettle Village
Box 380
Intercourse, PA 17534
(800) 732-3538
(717) 768-8261

Everything from this Pennsylvania Dutch purveyor is first-rate, from their
peach and pear fruit butters to jellies in surprising flavors, including Apple
Elderberry and Red Beet. It's all very wholesome and delicious.

Kozlowski Farms
5566 Gravenstein Highway
Forestville, CA 95436
(707) 887-1587

Try their Pink Grapefruit Marmalade or one of the Kozlowski family's other
dozen low-sugar jams and jellies, especially the rich-tasting berry flavors. A
good source for fruit vinegars such as raspberry and blueberry that can
liven up salad or serve as a marinade.

Wax Orchards
22744 Wax Orchards Road S.W.
Vashon Island, WA 98070
(800) 634-6132
(206) 682-8251

Truly a miraculous product line—fruit-sweetened dessert sauces that
include a thick fudge topping with only 16 calories per teaspoon. Also **try**
their Amaretto Fudge and ambrosial Orange Passion Fudge. **Wax Orchards**
makes an entire line of syrups, fruit butters, and chutneys, but their
dessert sauces are absolutely unbelievable.

Cinnabar Chutney
1134 W. Haining Street, Shop C
Prescott, AZ 86301
(602) 778-3687

I purchase all my Indian chutneys through Cinnabar in gallon-size jars
because I would never dare run out. Their Tomato Chutney sounds ordinary but sings on the palate; the Pear Cardamon Chutney is beyond com-
pare. Cinnabar also manufactures Jamaican Jerk Sauce and **Thai Tamarind**
Seafood Marinade and is constantly coming up with new, exciting products.

New Orleans School of Cooking
620 Decatur Street
New Orleans, LA 70130
(504) 482-3632

One-stop shopping for every Creole sauce and condiment, including many seldom seen outside Louisiana. The owners, Joe and Karen Cahn, manufacture their own line of spices called "Joe's Stuff," and they also carry the entire line of Paul Prudhomme products. If you're a fan of New Orleans style cooking (Cajun or Creole), this is the place to let the good eating times roll.

Carol's Chutney
5555 S.W. Childs Road
Lake Oswego, OR 97035
(503) 620-0164

Owner Carol Perlstein offers a large variety of savory chutneys in hearty Pacific Northwest flavors like Apple-Pear-Jalapeño and Cranberry Walnut. Harvest Hazelnut is my personal favorite as a condiment for turkey at holiday times.

Cookbooks and Videos

The Complete Book of Sauces
by Sally Williams

Light Sauces: Delicious Low Fat Low Cholesterol Recipes for Meats and Fish
by Barry Bluestein and Kevin Morrissey

The Sauce Bible
by David Paul Larousse

Sauces: Classics in Contemporary Saucemaking
by James Peterson

Sauces and Dressings: 84 Light and Easy Recipes
by Diane Rozas

Saucing Foods
by Deidre Davis

Stocks and Sauces
Cooking at the Academy Videos
California Culinary Academy
(800) 229-2433 ext. 232

INDEX

Italic indicates a sauce recipe